Karin Dalhues

Treehugging 2.0

Powerful Niche Media in the Battle for a Better Future?

Anchor Academic Publishing

Dalhues, Karin: Treehugging 2.0: Powerful Niche Media in the Battle for a Better Future? Hamburg, Anchor Academic Publishing 2013

Buch-ISBN: 978-3-95489-117-7
PDF-eBook-ISBN: 978-3-95489-617-2
Druck/Herstellung: Anchor Academic Publishing, Hamburg, 2013

Bibliografische Information der Deutschen Nationalbibliothek:
Die Deutsche Nationalbibliothek verzeichnet diese Publikation in der Deutschen Nationalbibliografie; detaillierte bibliografische Daten sind im Internet über http://dnb.d-nb.de abrufbar.

Bibliographical Information of the German National Library:
The German National Library lists this publication in the German National Bibliography. Detailed bibliographic data can be found at: http://dnb.d-nb.de

All rights reserved. This publication may not be reproduced, stored in a retrieval system or transmitted, in any form or by any means, electronic, mechanical, photocopying, recording or otherwise, without the prior permission of the publishers.

Das Werk einschließlich aller seiner Teile ist urheberrechtlich geschützt. Jede Verwertung außerhalb der Grenzen des Urheberrechtsgesetzes ist ohne Zustimmung des Verlages unzulässig und strafbar. Dies gilt insbesondere für Vervielfältigungen, Übersetzungen, Mikroverfilmungen und die Einspeicherung und Bearbeitung in elektronischen Systemen.

Die Wiedergabe von Gebrauchsnamen, Handelsnamen, Warenbezeichnungen usw. in diesem Werk berechtigt auch ohne besondere Kennzeichnung nicht zu der Annahme, dass solche Namen im Sinne der Warenzeichen- und Markenschutz-Gesetzgebung als frei zu betrachten wären und daher von jedermann benutzt werden dürften.

Die Informationen in diesem Werk wurden mit Sorgfalt erarbeitet. Dennoch können Fehler nicht vollständig ausgeschlossen werden und die Diplomica Verlag GmbH, die Autoren oder Übersetzer übernehmen keine juristische Verantwortung oder irgendeine Haftung für evtl. verbliebene fehlerhafte Angaben und deren Folgen.

Alle Rechte vorbehalten

© Anchor Academic Publishing, Imprint der Diplomica Verlag GmbH
Hermannstal 119k, 22119 Hamburg
http://www.diplomica-verlag.de, Hamburg 2013
Printed in Germany

Abstract

The environmental blogosphere – the entirety of blogs with a thematic focus on environmental issues – is the modern environmentalists' platform to inform and mobilise audiences. Against the backdrop of an increased presence of environmental issues in current public debates, this study compares the German and the UK environmental blogospheres in order to advance an understanding of their distinctive structures and contents. This research aim was met through a comprehensive review of literature, as well as through primary research on a total of 800 blog entries from German and UK environmental blogs. The research method of choice was content analysis, but also an adapted version of grounded theory was applied to one element of research. The key findings this study produced include that the dominant thematic foci strongly differ between the two countries and that UK bloggers express their opinions more strongly than German ones. Paradoxically, the German environmental movement appeared to be stronger than the UK one in general, but the UK environmental blogosphere in turn seemed to be more capable in using blogs as a platform for lobbying. Concerning structural blog features, which include for example entry length and number of comments, the study found that the differences between the two countries are rather small, but that there are significant discrepancies with earlier structural blog research, pointing towards a rapid development of blogs over the past years. The study concludes that, although the UK environmental blogosphere is more developed than the German one, there is a lot of potential for both countries' environmental movements to increase their power through blogging if they manage to blog more professionally and capture a larger readership.

Table of Contents

ABSTRACT V
TABLE OF CONTENTS VI
LIST OF FIGURES 1
LIST OF ABBREVIATIONS 2
1. INTRODUCTION 9
   1.1. Research Focus 9
   1.2. Structure of the Study 11
2. LITERATURE REVIEW 12
   2.1. Introduction 12
   2.2. Blogs and the Blogosphere 12
   2.3. Environmentalism 17
   2.4. Methodological Models 21
   2.5. Research Aim and Objectives 22
3. METHODOLOGY 24
   3.1. Research Strategy 24
   3.2. Ensuring the quality of the work 29
   3.3. Ethical Aspects 31
4. FINDINGS OF THE PRIMARY RESEARCH 32
   4.1. Blog Categories 33
   4.2. Length of Entries 35
   4.3. Reader Comments 36
   4.4. Links to External Sources 36
   4.5. Number of Authors 37
   4.6. Purpose of the Blog 37
   4.7. Blogs and Opinion 38
   4.8. Relative Significance of the Environmental Blogosphere 39
   4.9. Summary of Findings 40
   4.10. Conclusion 41
5. DISCUSSION AND SYNTHESIS OF THE FINDINGS 42
   5.1. Analysis of Blog Structures 42
   5.2. Miscellaneous Factors 53
6. CONCLUSIONS 57
   6.1. Research Objectives: Summary of Findings and Conclusions 57
   6.2. Recommendations for Further Research 60
   6.3. Contribution to Knowledge 63
   6.4. Limitations of the Study 64
APPENDIX I: REFERENCES 65
APPENDIX II: RESEARCH JOURNAL 70
APPENDIX III: RAW DATA FROM PRIMARY RESEARCH (PER BLOG) 69

List of Figures

Figure 1: Blog Categories Germany 34
Figure 2: Blog Categories UK 34
Figure 3: Average Length of Blog Entries in Words 35
Figure 4: Average Number of Links per 1,000 Words of Text 37
Figure 5: Average Use of "I" per 1,000 Words of Text 38
Figure 6: Top 20 General Blog Categories Germany 39
Figure 7: Top 20 General Blog Categories UK 40
Figure 8: The 5D Model of professor Geert Hofstede 46

List of Abbreviations

Abbreviation	Meaning
Defra	Department for Environment, Food and Rural Affairs of the United Kingdom
EC	European Community
EU	European Union
MP	Member of Parliament
NGO	Non-governmental organization
OECD	Organization for Economic Co-operation and Development
PR	Public Relations
SPD	Sozialdemokratische Partei Deutschlands (Social Democratic Party of Germany)
UK	United Kingdom of Great Britain and Northern Ireland
US / USA	United States of America

1. Introduction

In the course of the first decade of the twenty-first century, the internet has become an integral part of our everyday lives and has changed the way we communicate with each other. The internet has lifted public self-expression to a new level that the "old" mass-media such as television or newspapers could not provide (e.g. Gerhards and Schäfer, 2010, Huang et al., 2007).

One of the most prominent ways to express oneself on the web is by keeping a weblog, or "blog" as it is mostly referred to nowadays. Blogs are defined here as regularly updated online diaries (Herring et al., 2004b) and can fulfil a variety of purposes which will be discussed in chapter 2. Anyone with internet access has the opportunity to start a blog. Blogging started out in the USA, soon followed by the UK, which was one of the first European countries to have widespread high-speed internet available, along with other countries, amongst which Germany (Pedersen and Macafee, 2007b).

While the online community was watching how the blogosphere, the entirety of blogs, grew to proportions that can only be vaguely estimated, issues like climate change and an increasing public awareness for environmental affairs that came hand in hand with it arose and started to capture societies' attention.

Not surprisingly, people also started to blog about environmental issues, which was the hour of birth of the environmental blogosphere.

1.1. Research Focus

Yet, despite of the growing importance of environmental issues, no research specific to the environmental blogosphere has been conducted up to now. Against the background of a united Europe, which slowly merges the different cultures that it comprises, and in order to contribute to an otherwise rather US-centric research angle (Pedersen and Macafee, 2007b), the study at hand will provide an Anglo-German view on the environmental blogosphere. It will thus deliver valuable insights for a range of academic disciplines, principally to blog research and cultural research.

The research will take the shape of a comparative study, because some results only reveal their full explanatory power when seen in unison in two different countries, or, precisely when they stand in contrast to findings from other countries, which stimulates further research into the reasons for differing results.

Germany and the UK depict very suitable countries for a comparative study, because although they have many things in common, such as being powerful players in the European Union (EU) and being geographically close to each other, there are also significant differences between them. The UK is an

Anglophone country and therefore has had a head start in computer and internet technology, which is dominated by English language. The UK also has a closer relationship than Germany to the USA, which dominate and influence other countries in many ways, including blogging. Germany and the UK are thus two highly interesting countries to compare. Briefly summarised, the **aim of the research** can be phrased as:

> *To advance an understanding of the distinctive characteristics of the German as well as the UK environmental blogosphere in terms of structure and content*

In order to reach the research aim, it was felt necessary to find out more about environmentalism in the two countries and also to be clear about the nature of blogging and what is already known about it concerning the two countries. Without investigation of these two issues prior to the specific research into the environmental blogosphere, the results could have been misinterpreted. Understanding the differences between Germany and the UK in environmentalism and blogging separately was the basis for understanding them in combination - the environmental blogosphere. This knowledge was gained by performing a critical literature review. Only then, primary data was collected from a sample of German and UK environmental blogs, largely sticking to techniques that had been successful in previous blog studies, such as word counts. Finally with the backgrounds of blogging and environmentalism still in mind, conclusions could be drawn from the data gained from environmental blogs and the impacts of the results could be evaluated.

To summarise the above, the four **research objectives** which guided the research process are:

1. Identify how environmental movements have developed in Germany and the UK and assess their current state
2. Evaluate critically relevant knowledge on central features and characteristics of blogs in general, as well as blogs in Germany and the UK in particular
3. Explore and compare features of the German and the UK environmental blogosphere in terms of structure and content
4. Formulate an accurate snapshot of the current state of the German and UK environmental blogosphere and illustrate the implications of the findings

The objectives 3 and 4 evolved as a result of the critical literature review, but have been anticipated here for the convenience of the reader.

1.2. STRUCTURE OF THE STUDY

The first step to comparing the two countries was to collect general information on environmental movements in Germany and the UK as well as previous research results on blogging (objectives 1 and 2). This secondary data will be presented in the shape of a literature review in chapter 2. However, it was also found necessary to collect primary data in order to meet objective 3, whereby content analysis has been chosen as the most suitable research method for this kind of study, as it has proven effective in similar studies before (e.g. Herring et al., 2004a, Papacharissi, 2007, Zhou, 2009). It has been performed on the 20 top-ranked German as well as UK environmental blogs using a ranking provided by the website Wikio. Nevertheless, the research also contains elements of grounded theory. Chapter 3 provides more detailed information on research methodology and a justification of the choice of research instruments. The findings and discussion of the primary research will be presented in the chapters 4 and 5. The conclusions that were drawn from primary and secondary data are presented in chapter 6, which also suggests issues for further research and points out the limitations of the research project.

2. Literature Review

2.1. INTRODUCTION

Analysing blogs has become a popular research topic amongst academics, because the nature of blogs makes it easy to analyse them. They are in text form and the majority of bloggers keeps older posts in archives which are rarely modified or deleted. For this research the focus was on the top 20 German and UK environmental blogs.

The literature review is divided into three parts: blogs and the blogosphere, environmentalism and finally methodological models and research objectives. The section on blogs mainly deals with defining what a blog is, how blogs evolved, previous research done on blogs and the importance of blogging in Germany and the UK. The section on environmentalism provides a definition of what is meant by environmentalism in the context of this study, the history of environmentalism as well as its current state in Germany and the UK. The methodological models section 2.4. presents an overview of possible ways of researching blogs and illustrates them with examples from past research. Finally, the research objectives are developed as a result of previous research undertaken and presented in the literature review. The exact research methodology applied to this research will be explained in chapter 3.

2.2. BLOGS AND THE BLOGOSPHERE

2.2.1. What Is a Blog?

The starting point of this research about the German and UK blogosphere was the definition of what a blog is. The term has evolved from the word weblog and blogs are defined by Susan C. Herring, who has conducted various pieces of research about blogs and enjoys big credibility among academics, as "frequently modified webpages containing individual entries displayed in reverse chronological sequence" (Herring et al., 2004b). In 2002, the blogger William Quick proposed to call "the intellectual cyberspace [the] bloggers occupy: the *Blogosphere*" (Quick, 2002). For this study, the term "environmental blogosphere" will be used frequently. By environmental blogosphere the segment of the blogosphere which covers environmental issues is meant.

It is typical for blogs to provide links to other blogs and websites in their posts and in the so-called blogroll, which is a list of other blogs a blogger considers worth reading. This way, by linking to each others' blogs, a network with powerful and influential blogs in the centre and other blogs surrounding them is created (Tremayne, 2007b). It is also common for blogs to enable their readers to leave comments beneath blog entries, which encourages discussions and active participation by the readers (Mishne and Glance, 2006). There are both single-authored and multiple-authored blogs.

2.2.2. Who Uses Blogs and Why?

Blogs, as opposed to traditional media, are personal journals in which information gatekeeping does not occur to the extent it does in traditional media; bloggers can use their audience as a source, but also themselves, which researchers suspect to be one of the main attractions of blogging (Sundar et al., 2007). Reasons and motivations for blogging can generally be described as autobiographical reporting, commentary, catharsis, muse and community forum (Nardi et al., 2004). Blogs can thus function as internal information filters (e.g. personal journals), external information filters (e.g. world news) or appear in hybrid forms (Ko et al., 2008).

Other researchers, such as Blood (2002) use similar terms for blog categories such as filter blogs, personal journals and notebooks as the hybrid form. The German scholar Schönberger (2008) also adds knowledge blogs for collective knowledge management and blogs for marketing purposes to the above mentioned categories. Previous research suggests that around one third of blogs have a journalistic (filter) background, while two thirds are personal journals (Herring et al., 2004a). Schönberger (2008) criticises that despite being the minority of weblogs, scientific research predominantly focuses on the analysis of filter blogs.

As the blogs for marketing purposes demonstrate, blogs need not be personal or private in all cases. Also many businesses, politicians and organisations of all kinds engage in blogging. It is used as a means of public relations in order to establish relationships with stakeholders such as clients, employees, the voting public or the media. The goals of blogging for non-personal reasons can include for instance positioning one's organisation as a thought leader or giving a human face to a large corporation (Weber, 2009).

2.2.3. The Internet as a Public Sphere

The concept of the *blogosphere* has frequently been discussed in relation to Habermas' work about the transformation of the public sphere in which he describes the desirable public sphere as "an ideal democratic space for rational debate among informed and engaged citizens, a space that would thus be an arena mediating between state and society" (Rettberg, 2008:46). In his piece of work, Habermas (1990) illustrates how the bourgeois public sphere reached its peak in the 18th and 19th century in Europe; during this period of time the educated upper class of society engaged in rational-critical debates which Habermas considers the key feature of the public sphere and as an important pillar for true democracy. However, this feature vanished due to structural and economic changes, especially the evolution of mass media and society consequently became an accumulation of private people instead of a public space, merely "consuming" culture instead of creating and debating it, according to Habermas. Nowadays there are discussions to what extent the internet and the blogosphere represent Habermas' vision of the ideal public sphere.

The internet seems to bring back elements of participation and to some extent even out the imbalance of information flow between mass media and the audience, which is now able to participate again instead of solely consuming information (Habermas, 2008). However, Habermas concludes that the internet is still lacking an important element of the ideal public sphere, namely structures which absorb information published by internet users and which re-publish that information in a synthesised way. Gerhards and Schäfer (2010), who also conducted research about the internet as an ideal public sphere, come to the conclusion that there are no significant differences in participation and representation of non-influential individuals or groups on the internet compared to mass media, which, in their opinion, indicates that the internet is not a better public sphere. They also point to the fact that search engines are gatekeepers of information on the internet and that they can be manipulated by the powerful groups and networks on the internet so that the minorities again find it hard to draw attention to their publications, because they do not appear in good positions in search engine rankings.

However, there are also discussions taking place with one of the arguments being that blogging is seen by many bloggers merely as a means of personal communication with friends, family or colleagues instead of communication with a broader public. This questions the significance of the debate about blogging in relation to the public sphere, since many bloggers do not seek to be part of any public sphere at all (i.e. Schönberger, 2008).

The debate continues to the present day, but does not heavily influence the focus of this study, although when discussing the results of the research, the topic will be brought up again when comparing the German and the UK blogosphere (see chapter 5).

2.2.4. History of Blogs

The precursors of what we know as blogs today appeared in the late 1990's and the new technology became popular rapidly with the number of new blogs growing exponentially over the years (Herring et al., 2007a). Defining the current number of blogs is virtually impossible, but it can be considered a certainty that there are tens of millions (Caslon Analytics, 2009).

Blogs and the blogosphere have continued to become increasingly important and influential. An example which illustrates the rising influence of blogs is a bet between the blogger Dave Winer and New York Times journalist Martin Nisenholtz. In 2002 Winer bet the following and won: "In a Google search of five keywords or phrases representing the top five news stories of 2007, weblogs will rank higher than the New York Times' Web site" (Winer and Nisenholtz, 2002). Especially political blogs exert influence on various mainstream media (Tremayne, 2007b) and thus ultimately on the public opinion, though it needs to be kept in mind that research in this area focuses mainly on the US blogosphere.

After skyrocketing in the early years of the new millennium, the growth of the blogosphere is now slowing down, along with the number of blog entries published on a daily basis, which some consider a good development, as it leads to a professionalization of blogging, with less people starting a new blog and more abandoning their blog (Cheng, 2008). However, looked at from the perspective of the internet as a public sphere (see previous section) this is a negative sign, as the remaining bloggers are becoming more powerful gatekeepers, making it hard for new bloggers to make themselves heard (or read) in the public (blogo)sphere.

2.2.5. Research on Blogging

While the research about the US blogosphere is already quite advanced thanks to researchers such as Herring, comparatively little research has been conducted on the UK (Pedersen and Macafee, 2007b) and especially on Germany. Technorati, the largest search engine and index for weblogs, publishes annual reports about the state of the blogosphere. The latest report published in November 2010 shows that the biggest proportion of blogs worldwide (49%) is based in the US. The European Union accounts for 29% of the total amount of blogs (Sobel, 2010). Considering the volume of US blogs and the significance of the US as a nation it seems logic that it has been in the focus of research, but also research about other countries' blogospheres is slowly developing. There has for instance been research on the Chinese blogosphere (Zhou, 2009), the Irish blogosphere (Lee and Bates, 2007) or the Polish blogosphere (Trammell et al., 2006). Research about Germany and the UK will be introduced in the following sections.

There are three main academic disciplines which are interested in blog research. While for media theorists, the main focus of research is the extent to which blogs pose a challenge to traditional media, computer scientists develop algorithms to automatically collect information on public opinion for market research and sociologists are interested in blogger communities and motivations for blogging (Thelwall, 2006). The piece of research at hand contributes to the sociological research angle.

In the sociological field, blog research often focuses on political blogs (i.e. Goode, 2009, Zhou, 2009, Etling et al., 2010), which is also true for country-specific research for Germany (i.e. Ott, 2006) and the UK (i.e. Jackson, 2006, Dale, 2010b). However, since environmentalism is an increasingly significant topic for public debate, as it will be demonstrated later in this chapter, the author believes that research should be intensified in this field.

2.2.6. Blogging in Germany

According to previous research, blog use and influence in Germany can be considered rather low despite Germany being a technologically advanced country with the highest number of internet users in Europe (Kloppe, 2010). Kloppe also states that the number of blogs in German language is estimated to be between 200,000 and 500,000. These also include Austrian and Swiss blogs in German language. This implies that the blog readership is significantly lower than that of other Western countries, such as the UK, as it will be demonstrated in the next section. According to a 2006 study, Kloppe argues further, two-thirds of German bloggers interviewed stated to cover political issues.

The German media scholar Neuberger confirms this in a radio interview (Deutschlandfunk, 2011) saying that blogging in Germany is much less professionalised than for example in the United States. He explains that in other countries, blogs form a sort of counterweight to the daily press. Neuberger admits that it is not entirely clarified yet why there is no such development in Germany, but he says that many experts believe that the German press is good enough for a counterweight to be redundant. Neuberger also mentions that bloggers and blog readers in Germany form something like an "insider circle which enjoys dealing with itself", thus forming a somewhat elitist community. This statement is supported both by Kloppe's (2010) argument mentioned above saying that the blog readership is rather small and by Gerhards' and Schäfer's (2010) findings about the internet not being a better public sphere.

In summary it can be said that blogging is not a central component of the media system in Germany and is in all likelihood considered merely a hobby by many bloggers. Nevertheless, there are many thousands of blogs in Germany and this has not been done justice yet by researchers considering that there is still relatively little research on blogging in Germany.

2.2.7. Blogging in the United Kingdom

Concerning the situation in the UK, researchers point out that, although blogging seems to be more popular in the UK than in Germany, the significance of blogging in the UK is still much lower than in the US, the front-runners of the blogosphere, and so far no UK blogger is able to make a living from blogging (Dale, 2008).

It is virtually impossible to determine the exact number of blogs in the UK which is partly due to the fact that English is spoken worldwide and so the language a blog is written in cannot provide enough evidence to determine that a blog is from the UK. Nevertheless, Pedersen and Macafee (2007b) cite sources which estimate that there were 2.5 million bloggers in the UK in 2005 (Riley, 2005, cited in Pedersen and Macafee, 2007b), which, according to another source equals around 7% of the UK internet users (Office of Communications, 2006, cited in Pedersen and Macafee, 2007b). It can be assumed that the number of blogs has grown even further by now.

Dale (2008) stresses that mainstream media, such as The Daily Telegraph, The Guardian or The Spectator, also attempt to keep successful blogs, mostly of political nature. However, most of them are still struggling to find an audience comparable in size to the audiences of the UK top political blogs kept by citizens.

In a nutshell, it can be seen that there are far more blogs in the UK than in Germany and that in terms of development, the UK ranges somewhere between Germany and the US, probably closer to the US. Despite all similarities with the US blogosphere, the UK blogosphere is not yet very well researched, but researchers are busy changing that and this study will contribute yet another puzzle piece.

After the concepts of blogging and its respective popularity in Germany and the UK have been illuminated, the following sections will broach the issue of environmentalism.

2.3. ENVIRONMENTALISM

For the purpose of this study, environmentalism will be looked at in its broadest sense. As it will be clarified later, the most popular blogs with the environment as their main theme often either deal with niche topics of environmentalism or with various different topics, some of which do not necessary count as "environmental".

According to Marangudakis (2001) there are two concepts of environmentalism that need to be distinguished. The first one is anthropocentric and thus regards environmental protection as a necessity for welfare of the society. The second one however is ecocentric, with humanity being in the role of worshippers of the supreme Nature, which sometimes is also referred to Mother Earth, Great Being of Life or Gaia.

This study will focus on the anthropocentric meaning of environmentalism, the one that puts society in the centre, because all environmental blogs that were analysed deal with this type of environmentalism.

2.3.1. Environmental Movements

Environmental movements exist in various forms, but the core belief all movements share is the ability of humans to change aspects of the biophysical environment in order to eliminate or minimise the effects they have on things that humans care about (Stern et al., 1999). Stern et al. also distinguish movement activists and movement supporters, activists being the core of the movement, heavily involved in actions, while supporters sympathise with the movement and are prepared to take part in actions and give money in a more limited way than the activists. According to this distinction, it can be assumed that people who care to invest time in setting up an environmental blog are activists.

There are various reasons why people wish to protect the environment. Especially in the West, the fast development of cities, industry and materialism has lead to a "psychological angst" (Marangudakis, 2001:459) and that way fuelled the desire to get back to nature (Marangudakis, 2001). Just how far society has already moved away from nature is illustrated by an article published on the website of the German newspaper Süddeutsche Zeitung (Blawat, 2011) which states that German children, regardless whether they grew up on the countryside or in cities, have an inhibited relationship with nature. An interviewee who manages a nature conservancy centre criticises that children can report on climate change and explain terms like "Kyoto Protocol" while at the same time being scared of insects and climbing on trees.

Before taking a closer look at the environmental movement in Germany and the UK it will be specified a bit more what exactly is meant by "Germany" and "the UK".

2.3.2. Defining Germany and UK

When talking about the situation of the environmental movement in "Germany" between 1949 and 1990, this refers to the Federal Republic of Germany (West Germany) which was separated from the communist German Democratic Republic (East Germany) during that period of time. The Eastern German federal states were officially reunited with the West in October 1990. When referring to the environmental movement of "Germany" in the 1990's and beyond, the reunited Federal Republic of Germany in its current shape is meant.

When talking about the "UK" or "United Kingdom", the United Kingdom of Great Britain and Northern Ireland is meant, which has been in its current shape since 1922 when the Republic of Ireland became independent and only Northern Ireland remained part of the UK.

After clarifying which countries this study will address, the following sections will look at their involvement in environmentalism.

2.3.3. Environmentalism in Germany

Although conservative environmental movements had been around much longer, the modern environmental movement in Germany evolved in the late 1960's when a new generation of university students was seeking to break free from what had moved their parents' generation which had been heavily influenced by the Holocaust and the Second World War (Dryzek et al., 2003). The movement was strongly connected with the anti-nuclear and the peace movements that took place in the same period of time. However, politics excluded the anti-nuclear and the environmental movement from their agenda which led to an "oppositional counter-culture" (Dryzek et al., 2003:37) which in turn led to the German Green Party now having a programme that goes beyond addressing environmental issues. Rather, their programme is one of societal change in its entireness.

Once an offspring of the environmental movement of the late 1960's the German Green Party, founded in 1980, has been an important political player since it first entered the German parliament (Bundestag) in 1983 and certainly since it first formed a coalition with the social democrats (SPD) in 1998, thus actively participating in running the country.

Also in the new millennium environmental issues continue to be an important part of Germany's public policy and debates (OECD, 2001). A very current example is the success of the Green Party in the federal state of Baden-Württemberg where the party won the elections and appointed the first Green leader of a state parliament in Germany, this time having the social democrats as their smaller coalition partner. According to data presented by Spiegel Online (Der Spiegel, 2011), if there were general elections at the time of writing this report (summer 2011) it would be possible that Germany elected its first Green chancellor. Environmental issues that move Germany at the time of writing mostly deal with the future of energy supply, which involves Germany's nuclear phase-out (i.e. Süddeutsche, 2011) and the development of stable networks powered by renewable energy (i.e. Preuß, 2011).

2.3.4. Environmentalism in the UK

In the UK, the environmental movement has grown stronger only in recent years. While the environmental movement in Germany rose along with other movements in the late 1960's, some groups such as the Royal Society for the Protection of Birds had already existed for several decades then and unlike the German groups, those early UK environmentalist groups did not see themselves in opposition to the government, but were in fact collaborating, some of the groups even receiving royal patronage. Nevertheless, those groups hardly had any political influence and lobbying showed little effect (Dryzek et al., 2003). Only in the 1970's did the environment gain more importance in public, which can be traced, for example, through increased and regular coverage of environmental issues in *The Times* (Clapp, 1994). Still, the government refused to make major concessions to environmental claims and leaked documents dated to 1979 from Thatcher's term reveal that there were plans to reduce sensitivity for environmental concerns among the population. In the 1980's budget cuts further reduced environmental agencies' (e.g. Clean Air Council) power (Dryzek et al., 2003). Environmental issues were thus being actively excluded from the political agenda in the UK.

From the 1980's however, the European Community (EC) and later its successor, the European Union (EU), which the UK was (and continues to be) a member of, influenced environmental politics in the country. Environmental groups now had a new platform for lobbying in Brussels. During the 1990's UK politics opened up to moderate environmental groups, but continued to actively exclude groups they considered non-moderate. The Blair Government which was elected in 1997 seemingly engaged more in environmental issues and Deputy Prime Minister John Prescott was elected minister for the environment, which was to demonstrate the importance the government seemed to ascribe to the environment. However, despite some actions that the government took in environmental questions, the issue was still not on top of the political agenda (Dryzek et al., 2003).

The electoral system also complicated business for the Green Party in the UK. Despite achieving reasonable shares of votes the party could not gain any seats in parliament in the past. Only in the 1990's The Greens were able to gain more power when two members were elected to the European Parliament and one to the Scottish Assembly (Dryzek et al., 2003). The party separated in the 1990's and now consists of the sister parties Green Party of England and Wales, Green Party in Northern Ireland and Scottish Green Party (Green Party of England and Wales, 2011). On a national level the first green MP won a seat in parliament in the general elections of 2010 (BBC News, 2010).

Nowadays in the UK, public concerns about the environment and related issues are growing. Survey results published by the Department for Environment, Food and Rural Affairs (Defra) show that over the past years the knowledge about environmental issues has increased among the population and more people are willing to do things to help the environment, thus being potential movement supporters (Department for Environment Food and Rural Affairs, 2009).

2.3.5. Differences in Environmentalism between Germany and the UK

In summary it can be said that even though there were environmental groups much earlier in the UK than in Germany, their political influence remained and still remains limited. While political exclusion triggered a strong oppositional culture in Germany and the electoral system lifted the German Greens into power, environmental groups in the UK struggled to exert much influence on politics. The UK electoral system also prevented the Green Party from winning any seats in the national parliament for a long time. In 2010 the Green Party of England and Wales succeeded to have the first green MP elected to the national parliament while in Germany the first green leader of a federal state has assumed office and election forecasts for the next general election look bright for The Greens in Germany.

After the theory about blogs and environmentalism has been reviewed, the following section will introduce the approaches that previous studies have taken in order to conduct blog research.

2.4. Methodological Models

In order to assess which research techniques would be suitable for this study about environmental blogs previous studies on blogs have been critically evaluated. In terms of research methodology, earlier studies of the blogosphere have primarily made use of quantitative approaches such as content analysis.

Papacharissi (2007) for example performed some basic research using content analysis when there was still little research done on blogs and examined what characteristics were typical for blogs in terms of content, structure and design. She concluded that, at the time she was researching, blogs "presented low-tech, self-referential, verbose attempts to display personal thoughts and information, with little interest for how these thoughts would be received by an audience" (Papacharissi, 2007:37).

Susan C. Herring certainly is one of the pioneers and central researchers in the area of blog research. Her work is referred to in almost every piece of research about blogs and she has published multiple papers on different topics concerning the blogosphere. She makes use of content analysis frequently, for example in assessing to what extend blogs are interconnected (Herring et al., 2005a) or in performing a genre analysis of blogs (Herring et al., 2004a).

Besides general research introduced above, there has also been research on particular parts of the blogosphere. In the UK, Iain Dale researches political blogs (i.e. Dale, 2010a) and also the biblioblogosphere is a popular research subject (i.e. Kaden et al., 2007, Lee and Bates, 2007). Etling et al. (2010) provide an example for country-specific blog research, attempting to map the Arab blogosphere. Some of these researchers also made use of qualitative techniques, such as interviews, in order to gain insight into the blogosphere (i.e. Smith, 2010).

There have also been comparative studies before that analysed and compared blog data of two or more countries. Examples are a comparison of the German and the Chinese blogosphere conducted by He et al. (2007) using content analysis and a comparison of UK and US blogging practices by Pedersen and Macafee (2007a) who surveyed 120 bloggers.

The author believes that content analysis will also prove useful as the primary research method for the comparisons between German and UK blogs, because content analysis provides a simple and little error-prone way of research, when performed correctly. Further information about the research methodology applied to this study will be provided in the following chapter.

2.4.1. The Environmental Blogosphere – Uncharted Territory

As seen previously, the importance of environmental issues is increasing. In spite of that, to the knowledge of the author, no research on the environmental blogosphere has been published yet, even though blogs exert influence on public opinion and debate to a certain degree and could therefore manipulate societies' opinions on environmental issues and eventually change political actions and standpoints of a country. This study therefore aims at making an initial contribution to closing this gap of knowledge. Reviewing the literature led to the research aims and objectives, which have been introduced in chapter 1, but will be repeated here for the convenience of the reader.

2.5. RESEARCH AIM AND OBJECTIVES

The previously presented results of earlier research summarised in the literature review depict the first step to reaching the aim and objectives of this research project, which have already been introduced in chapter 1. To remind, the reader, the research aim and objectives were

Research aim:

> *To advance an understanding of the distinctive characteristics of the German as well as the UK environmental blogosphere in terms of structure and content*

Research objectives:

1. Identify how environmental movements have developed in Germany and the UK and assess their current state
2. Evaluate critically relevant knowledge on central features and characteristics of blogs in general, as well as blogs in Germany and the UK in particular
3. Explore and compare features of the German and the UK environmental blogosphere in terms of structure and content
4. Formulate an accurate snapshot of the current state of the German and UK environmental blogosphere and illustrate the implications of the findings

Objective 1 and 2 have been addressed in this chapter and the results for objective 3 will be presented in chapter 4. The final summary and conclusion for all objectives can be found in chapter 6. But first, in chapter 3 the research methodology will be explained.

3. Methodology

In this chapter, the research methodology is described. The primary scientific technique used to analyse the data was content analysis and this chapter provides information on the benefits and limitations of this technique as well as an explanation of the sampling and coding process and evaluations of reliability and validity of the research results. Additionally, an adapted version of grounded theory was applied, which will also be explained in detail in this chapter. The next chapter will then provide the findings of the content analysis.

3.1. RESEARCH STRATEGY

This study can be termed an empirical comparative study. "Empirical" denotes that the data has been collected through the use of human senses (Oliver, 2010) and can be applied to qualitative as well as quantitative research techniques. In this particular study data was predominantly collected through quantitative, statistical observations in the shape of content analysis and partly by using grounded theory.

The subjects of comparison of this study are the German and the UK environmental blogosphere. Comparative studies can be problematic, because often variables to be analysed differ between countries which makes them harder to compare, but nonetheless there is an increased demand for this type of research against the backdrop of European integration as well as globalisation (Clasen, 1999). In order to make the figures from the content analysis comparable between both countries, the calculations have been performed using percentages or per mills. This will be explained in more detail in the following section.

3.1.1. Content Analysis

This research has made use of content analysis, a technique which is thought to be "the fastest-growing technique in quantitative research" (Neuendorf, 2002:1), although there are also researchers who regard content analysis as a qualitative technique (Harris, 2001). It is valued for yielding objective data through counting, thanks to data collection taking place according to pre-defined "explicit rules" (Berg, 1998:224, cited in Harris, 2001:193).

Riffe et al. (1998) regard replicability and quantification as the central strengths of content analysis, but also acknowledge that these are often the main points of criticism of using content analysis, because, if not used correctly, it can lead to superficial research results. Holsti (1969:10, cited in Riffe et al., 1998:29) has called it "precision at the cost of problem significance". The superficiality criticism is fortified by content analysis' intention to interpret the manifest meaning of content, which is the linguistically denotative meaning. Critics argue that it neglects the latent, between-the-lines meaning of content. However, Riffe et al. (1998) challenge this argument by pointing out that manifest meanings can be interpreted without having to talk to the communicators or receivers. Besides, if there are multiple coders, the manifest meaning is the only one that is largely objective and judged equally by the coders.

Generally, being a quantitative technique, content analysis can be assumed to be more transparent, to deliver more objective results than a qualitative technique and to be easier to replicate and generalise (Daymon, 2002). For the research presented here, objectivity was one of the main goals and the numeric analysis had proven very suitable in related previous research (see Chapter 2.4.).

Nevertheless, in order to yield the desired results, research needs to be planned carefully. Harris (2001:194) suggests eight steps for performing content analyses:

1) Identify the questions to be asked and constructs to be used
2) Choose the texts to be examined
3) Decide on the size or type of response to be counted in the analysis, the so-called "unit of analysis"
4) Determine the categories into which the responses are to be divided
5) Generate the coding scheme
6) Conduct a sample or pilot study and revise the categories and coding scheme as needed
7) Collect the data
8) Assess validity and reliability, having earlier reviewed how validity can be enhanced and assessed

These steps have been followed and will be described in more detail in the following sections of this chapter. Several pilot studies (see step 6) have been conducted and consequently the process started again at step 3 until the resulting data sets seemed suitable to answer the research questions which evolved from coding (see also section 3.1.3.).

3.1.2. Sampling and Coding

For the research project 20 popular blogs about environmental topics were analysed. In order to figure out which blogs were most popular in Germany and the UK, a ranking by the website Wikio has been used. Wikio has also been used in previous studies, such as Dale (2010b), Schall and Müller (2011) and Torres-Zúñiga (2009) and was therefore considered a valid source. Next to that, Wikio is one of the few platforms that provide rankings for several countries. By using a single platform to obtain rankings for two countries it could be ensured that the algorithms according to which the ranking was created were the same for both samples. This adds *reliability* to the study, which will be discussed more closely in section 3.2.1

Some blogs were excluded from the sample because they did not show the typical features of a blog which have been discussed in chapter 2. The sample consisting of 20 blogs each from Germany and the UK was thus actually taken from the top 30 of the Wikio ranking.

From each of the 20 sampled blogs the latest 20 entries including comments were collected. Data collection took place on the 1st, 2nd and 4th of July 2011. The latest posts included are therefore posted on the 4th of July and any comments made after that date were not included in the data analysis. This resulted in 400 German blog entries and 400 UK blog entries plus comments. All blog entries and comments were saved locally on a computer so that potential amendments made by the bloggers at a later point in time would not bias the research. The *units of research* were thus the blog entries.

During data analysis a distinction has also been made between single-authored and multi-authored blogs as well as private and non-personal blogs (see also chapter 4). Non-personal blogs include corporate blogs, blogs of NGOs and other types of organisations as well as blogs of politicians, which were only found in the UK sample.

The coding categories were designed to deliver suitable data in accordance with research objective 3. Coding variables included number of authors, private or non-personal blog, blog category[1], number of links in post, number of comments per entry, number of words per entry excluding title and number of the personal pronoun "I" per 1,000 words (see Appendix II for coding instructions). Each of the variables has been analysed statistically according to the blog in itself and the country, so that comparisons could be made easily. In developing the codebook, previous blog research (see chapter 2.4.) has been used as a benchmark in order to identify good practice and come up with meaningful variables.

While the analysis of some variables, such as number of words or number of links, are purely quantitative and not very prone to human errors, establishing the different categories is more subjective with the author deciding the number and denotation of categories as well as placing blogs and blog entries into the categories. This process will be described closely in section 3.1.4. After establishing the categories though, a quantitative approach was used again to count and compare the number of blogs and blog entries in certain categories. Section 3.2. about ensuring the quality of the work will provide more details on this issue.

---

[1] Section 3.1.4 will provide detailed information on how the categories were established using grounded theory

3.1.3. Pilot Studies

Before the final data collection took place, a number of pilot studies with small samples were run which tested whether certain variables were suitable for analysis and would deliver useful data to draw conclusions from. Also, when more literature on the topic was found, some parameters of the study were altered so the resulting data could be compared to or add value to existing findings.

Initially it was planned to also include blogger demographics in the study, but the idea was dropped because only a small number of blogs provided demographic data and the small sample size could not be used to draw any conclusions on the total population.

The author also looked at blogs ranked beyond the top 30, but it turned out that the total number of environmental blogs is so small that after the top 30, most blogs were not very frequently updated anymore and there was hardly any user interaction to be observed there. This in itself was a conclusion already, to find out that, at least according to the Wikio rankings, the environmental blogosphere is only a niche sphere despite the increased significance of the issue in today's public debates as it has been seen in chapter 2.3.

Due to the small size of the environmental blogosphere, the sample of blogs was limited to 20 for each country, but the number of individual entries analysed on each blog was increased to 20 per blog, so that there would be 400 entries for each country to be analysed, which provided a suitable basis for statistic investigations, which also was in line with the study's time constraints.

3.1.4. Establishing Blog Categories Using Grounded Theory

Even though the primary research was performed using content analysis for the most part, it was found necessary to use a grounded-theory-like approach to establish the different blog categories which made it possible to compare the sampled blogs according to the particular topics they were covering.

While reading through the sampled blog entries, the author recognised that most blogs were specialised on one or more thematic areas within the range of environmental topics and decided that it would be valuable to compare the German and the UK blogosphere according to the topic areas they cover. However, Wikio, which had been used to identify the top-ranked environmental blogs, did not provide any sub-categories for the sampled blogs so that these needed to be created by the author herself.

A technique was used that strongly resembles grounded theory, which is a research technique that creates coding schemes and theories from already existing data instead of analysing data according to pre-defined schemes as it is done with many other research techniques (Allan, 2003). In applying grounded theory there are four stages as defined by Glaser and Strauss (1967, cited in Allan, 2003) who invented this research technique in the 1960's: Stage one is called *coding* and involves reading through the material and taking notes on the key points. In the second stage, by grouping similar codes, *concepts* emerge. Stage three further generalises the concepts into *categories*. Finally a *theory* is generated from the categories. The theory does not require further justification or testing because it emerged from the live data.

To quote Dr. David Douglas (2003:51), "the distinctive advantage of grounded theory is that it commences from specific 'grounded in reality' situations [...] with the intent of understanding the nature and rationale of observed incidents". Hence, it is free from preconceptions that could influence the research outcomes. However, developing grounded theory is a somewhat subjective approach and establishing blog categories might be difficult to replicate exactly the same way the author did. This in turn poses a threat to the reliability of the work (see also section 3.2.1. on reliability). Nevertheless there was no other research technique that could be used here due to time constraints. If the study was to be conducted again with more time capacities available, a more objective way to arrive at blog categories could involve statistic analyses of the most frequently used words or phrases in the blog entries which would lead to a more informed way of creating of categories which would yield a higher replicability.

In terms of research procedure, for this study the author first read through all blog entries and wrote down keywords which denoted the topic of the individual entry (stage one). Consequently all codes belonging to one blog were summarised in as few keywords as possible (stage two) before ultimately creating the final blog categories out of those keywords (stage three). Stage four was omitted, because the categories were the desired outcome of using grounded theory. The research technique has thus been used for purposes other than intended to a certain extent, but the fact that making use of stages one to three has yielded useful data in other research contexts make this altered use of grounded theory more reliable than inventing a new technique for establishing blog categories.

As mentioned before, calculations about the categories were made using statistical techniques again.

3.2. ENSURING THE QUALITY OF THE WORK

A piece of research can only make a meaningful contribution when its quality is ensured and possible limitations or flaws are acknowledged. For research in the field of communication, the most frequently used model used to identify the quality of research is that of reliability and validity (Daymon, 2002). Limitations of the study and reflection on it are discussed in chapter 6. Reliability and validity are addressed in the following sections.

3.2.1. Reliability

Daymon (2002:90) describes *reliability* as "the extent to which a research instrument [...], when used more than once, will re-produce the same results or answer".

For the particular research undertaken here, the concept of reliability has some flaws. The reasons for that are that the sample was not chosen randomly, so not every blog of the environmental blogosphere had the chance to be chosen for analysis. If replicated at a later point in time, the Wikio ranking that was used for choosing the sample might have changed and different blogs could end up in the sample. Furthermore, the latest 20 entries were collected for analysis, which would also yield a different set of data if the study was to be replicated at a later point in time.

However, since the internet is a fast-moving medium, this piece of research should be regarded as a "snapshot" of the situation at the time of writing. In order to be able to judge the developments over time, several studies with the same setup should be conducted and in this case it is explicitly desired that future research does *not* yield exactly the same results, because the changes in the blogosphere are what researchers are looking for in order to follow the evolution of blogs (Herring et al., 2005b).

If however, the study was conducted again with the same sample and the same data set, it would be easily replicable and result in the same data for the content analysis, which demonstrates the objectivity of the researcher. The research journal provided in Appendix II supports this statement. The only part of the research that depended on human judgement, and is therefore a potential threat to reliability is the categorisation of blogs using grounded theory, as already discussed in chapter 3.1.4.

3.2.2. Intercoder Reliability

Another issue that should be briefly addressed here is that of intercoder reliability. Particularly in content analysis it is important that the coders who analyse the data rate it as much in the same way as possible. When a high rating of intercoder reliability is calculated it can also function as one of several proves for the validity of the research (Lombard et al., 2002).

For this research project about the environmental blogospheres of Germany and the UK the author was the only coder and therefore intercoder reliability is not an issue. Nevertheless, strict coding rules have been applied as described in the research journal in Appendix II. Besides, many of the analyses, such as the word counts, were computer-aided which minimised the risk of human bias. Only in choosing which category a blog belonged to there would be a risk of inconsistent rating.

3.2.3. Validity

Validity assesses whether the research approach is suitable for researching a particular subject and whether the results can thus be plausible (Daymon, 2002). Daymon enlists three types of validity:

Internal validity deals with the extent to which findings are correct and reflect reality. In order to assess internal validity, readers of this study can consult the research journal (see Appendix II) which shows that the study has been constructed logically and coherently and an attempt was made to make it as transparent as possible so that there was little room for mistakes.

Another aspect of validity is the question whether findings can be *generalised* and whether the findings could be transferred to similar settings or populations. The research procedure could be easily used again for other countries' environmental blogospheres, especially countries that Wikio provides rankings for, but it cannot be assumed that there would be similar findings and, as explained in the previous section, this is not desired, because the research results depict a snapshot of a highly specialised and unique area of research. This is in line with claims by researchers such as Wolcott (1994) and Stake (1995) (both cited in Daymon, 2002) who also challenge the need for research to be generalisable.

The third aspect of validity is *relevance*, which scrutinises the importance and usefulness of the study for both the researcher and the readers. As already explained in the research proposal (see Appendix V) this study can contribute to both knowledge about the blogosphere of two countries and also cultural research for Germany, the UK and research in a European context. The research of German blogs in particular complies with other researchers' calls for research on non-English blogs (e.g. Herring et al., 2005b). Therefore, readers with various academic backgrounds can benefit from the research results. For the author of the study, the research offers an opportunity to gain additional knowledge in her field of study, which is communication, and it also provides information about the area the author would like to specialise in professionally, which is sustainability. It can thus be concluded, that relevance is ensured for this piece of research.

3.3. ETHICAL ASPECTS

Every researcher should be aware of research ethics, particularly when dealing with human participants. The blogs which have been examined are all publicly available on the internet and it can be assumed that the bloggers are aware of this and do not regard their blog entries as secret or confidential. Nevertheless, the bloggers are not aware that they have been part of a research project and therefore the author considered it fair not to mention the blogs by name, but merely provide the results of the content analysis anonymously (see Appendix III). This has also been done in order to protect the reader from being biased or offended by blog titles, which could have a negative effect on the perception of the research results.

4. Findings of the primary research

This chapter will summarise and present the findings from the primary research which has been performed on 800 blog entries in total. It will show differences and similarities between German and UK top-ranked environmental blogs, using a ranking by Wikio, as introduced in the previous chapter on methodology. Conclusions will be drawn from the data in the following chapter.

Before the results are presented however, the author would like to draw the reader's attention to a couple of factors that should be kept in mind when looking at the results:

As seen in the literature review, Germany seems to be lagging behind most other Western countries when it comes to blogging. It could also be seen there that the majority of German as well as UK blogs deal with politics. Environmental blogs are thus on the fringes of the blogosphere, although some of them specialise in the political aspect of sustainability and the environment.

The differences in size of the environmental blogospheres of Germany and the United Kingdom have to be taken into account when analysing the data gathered. The data was taken from a sample of 20 German and 20 UK environmental blogs and from each blog the 20 most recent entries were collected so that there was a total number of 800 blog entries that was analysed. The raw data can be found in Appendix III.

The data collected about the German and UK blogs was compared in terms of blog categories, length of entries, comments made by readers, number of links, number of authors and finally purpose of the blog (personal or non-personal; way of giving opinions). Although most blogs that were analysed did not provide figures about the size of their readership, calculations using percentages or per mills (per 1,000 words) made it possible to compare both blogospheres also in terms of user involvement. Furthermore, an attempt was made to assess the relative significance of the environmental blogosphere in the blogosphere as a whole.

The primary research which was conducted using content analysis and grounded theory, as described earlier, yielded the following data:

4.1. BLOG CATEGORIES

In order to compare the broad topic areas that the top-ranked German and British environmental blogs cover, categories have been established and all blogs from the sample have been assigned one or two categories. The categories have been established in a grounded-theory-like approach as described in section 3.1.4. of the previous chapter on methodology.

The definitions of the different categories are provided hereunder.

Parliamentary & Public Debates: blogs reporting about and/or commenting on parliamentary and other debates taking place in the public sphere (i.e. newspaper interviews, political talk shows) which deal with environmental topics. Examples of current debates include the debate on feed-in tariffs for renewable energy in the UK and Germany's nuclear power phase-out.

Activism: blogs that report on environmental activism taking place and trying to engage their audience to join and to become active. These blogs often belong to NGOs such as Greenpeace or the UK NGO Greener Leith.

Sustainable Lifestyle: blogs that deal with things every individual can do on the way towards a sustainable life on earth. Blogs in this category typically cover topics such as recycling and reusing, ecological food or green fashion.

Renewable Energy / Climate Change: blogs which cover issues related to climate change and how it can be tackled by producing renewable energy. The category includes blogs that deal with private production of renewable energy (e.g. solar panels on private home roofs), but also the macroeconomic implications of climate change.

The results look as follows[2]:

---

[2] As some blogs have been assigned two categories the percentages in both graphs add up to more than 100%

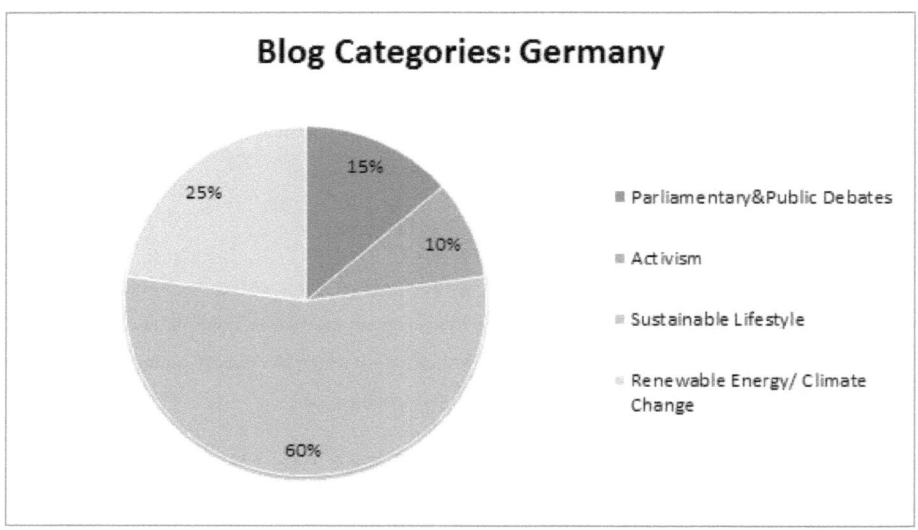

Figure 1: Blog Categories Germany

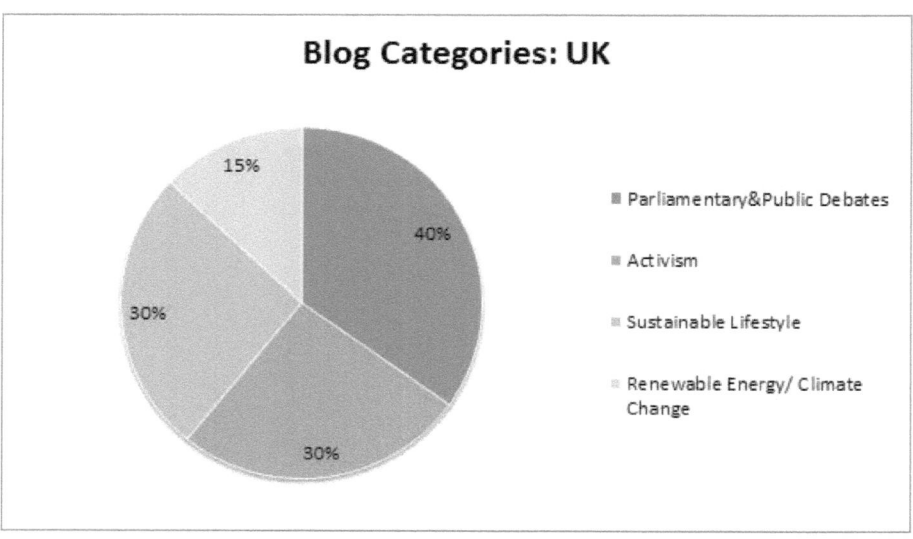

Figure 2: Blog Categories UK

The graphs show that top-ranked environmental blogs in the two countries have very different foci. While in Germany 60% of the blogs in the sample deal with sustainable lifestyle, that means, what every individual can do to contribute to a sustainable future, only 30% of the UK blogs deal with this topic. In the UK environmental blogosphere, the political aspect is most important, 40% of the blogs dealing with parliamentary and public debates about environmental topics. In Germany, only 15% of the blogs in the sample cover these kinds of issues related to environmentalism. Similarly, the category activism, which is closely related to the politically motivated debates, is more important in the UK (30%) than in Germany (15%). The topic renewable energy and climate change accounts for 25% on German blogs and 15% on UK blogs.

4.2. LENGTH OF ENTRIES

Concerning the average length of blog entries in words, data shows that UK blog entries tend to be slightly longer than German ones. While German entries had 371 words on average, UK entries had 77 words more on average (448).

However, there were big differences in individual blogs, some having as much as 800 words per entry on average while other had hardly 100 words. Nevertheless, it can be said that UK blogs had more blogs with long entries.

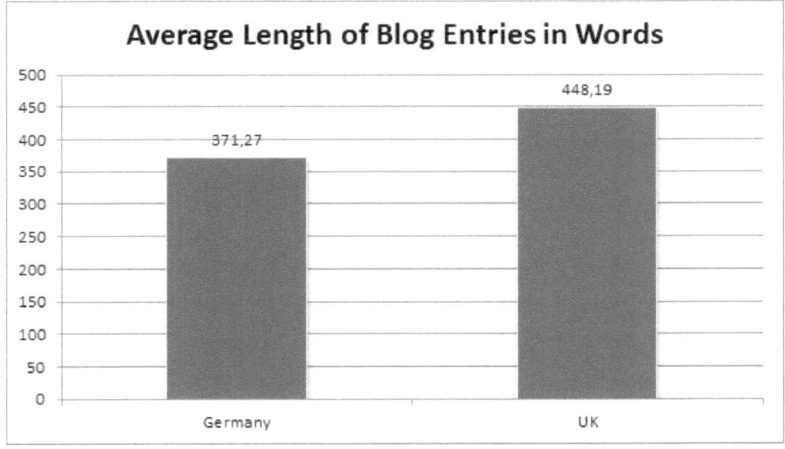

Figure 3: Average Length of Blog Entries in Words

4.3. READER COMMENTS

Besides a higher average of words per entry, UK blogs also seem to have more active readers who leave comments. The average number of comments in UK environmental blogs is almost twice as high (4.24 comments per entry on average) than on German environmental blogs (2.53 comments per entry on average). These figures might point either towards a higher number of readers or a more involved readership for the UK. This aspect will be looked at in depth in the next chapter.

However, in the UK sample there was one blog that had an extremely high number of comments compared to the rest of the sample, which significantly increased the average for the UK sample. Therefore, a second calculation has been performed for both samples using the median, which is another measure of centre technique that leaves outliers out of the calculation. The median for the UK sample was 1.28 and 1.13 for the German sample which shows that there is hardly any difference in the number of comments when leaving outliers out of the equation.

Another remarkable observation about the number of comments is that many entries did not have comments at all, which cannot be seen from the figures calculated above. 60.75 % of the German entries did not have any comments, while for the UK posts it was 50.0%. That means that those entries which have comments have relatively more comments on the UK environmental blogs. If the entries without comments are left out of the calculations, the German entries have 6.44 comments on average while the UK entries have 8.47 comments per entry on average.

It can thus be concluded that people leave more comments on the UK blogs, which goes for the amount of comments as well as the number of blog entries that receive comments at all. Nevertheless, the differences between the two countries are rather small.

4.4. LINKS TO EXTERNAL SOURCES

One of the characteristics of blogs is that in their entries they link to external sources, sometimes also to internal sources on the blog itself. In the sample the percentage of entries that did not contain any links at all is almost identical for Germany (14.0%) and the UK (13.75%). However, German entries provided more links on average, namely 13.64 links per 1,000 words of text, whilst the UK blogs only linked to 10.09 sources per 1,000 words.

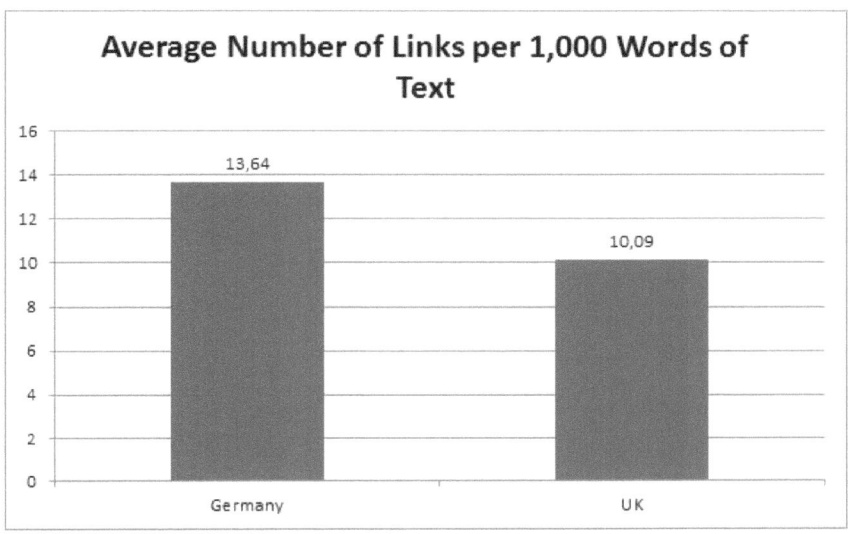

Figure 4: Average Number of Links per 1,000 Words of Text

4.5. NUMBER OF AUTHORS

Many blogs have more than one author. This was the case for 40% of the sample in both countries. Since each sample only contained 20 blogs, this number is not statistically valid to prove that this is true for the entire (environmental) blogosphere, but it indicates that there are no significant differences between Germany and the UK in this area.

4.6. PURPOSE OF THE BLOG

As mentioned in the literature review (see chapter 2), blogs can be kept for personal reasons, but also as a communication tool for companies, politicians, NGOs and other kinds of groups and organizations. 40% of the blogs in the German sample were non-personal. In the UK sample there were 60% non-personal blogs. In the UK blog sample, there were several politicians from the Green Party, while in the German sample there were no politicians at all. For both samples, it was mostly not obvious at first glance that blogs belonged to organizations. This could only be found out by reading the "about" page or something in the small print. The reasons why a blog may wish to conceal that it is non-personal are discussed in the following chapter.

4.7. BLOGS AND OPINION

A remarkable difference between German and UK environmental blogs seems to be that fact that blogging is used as a tool to express one's opinion to a bigger extent in the UK than in Germany. When reading through the entries that were sampled it became clear that especially blogs from the more political categories parliamentary & public debates and activism strongly reflected the authors' views. German blogs, although most of them could not be called objective, appeared to express opinions more subtle and German entries looked more like newspaper articles than like essays that express personal views.

This also shows in the statistical analysis, when comparing how many times the personal pronoun "I" is used in the blogs. In the UK sample, the word "I" was used 1,679 times, which results in an average number of 9.03 "I"'s per 1,000 words of text. In the German sample, the German equivalent for "I" was only found 893 times, which equals 5.80 "I"'s per 1,000 words.

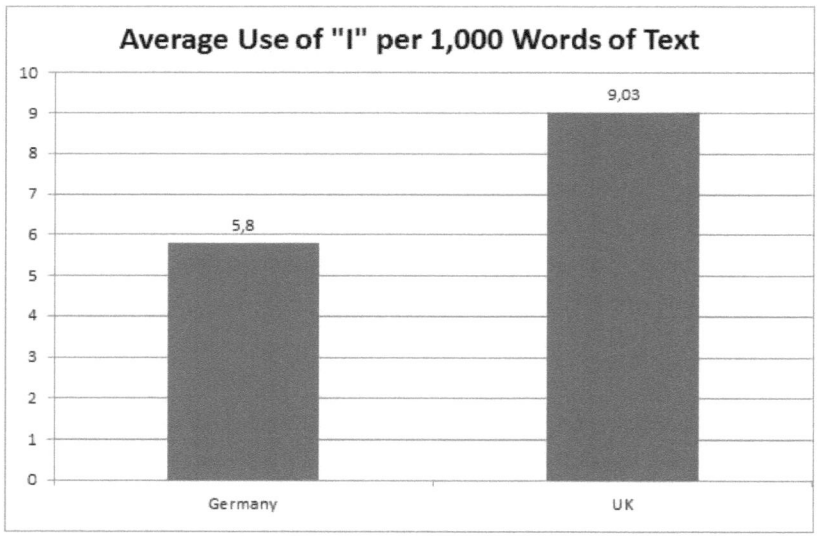

Figure 5: Average Use of "I" per 1,000 Words of Text

Investigation on why expressing personal views appears to be of greater importance in the UK will take place in the following chapter.

4.8. Relative Significance of the Environmental Blogosphere

How important are environmental topics in the blogosphere as a whole? In order to address this question, Wikio statistics have been analysed. Next to the ranking for environmental blogs, Wikio also publishes general rankings (see Appendix IV). The top-ranked UK environmental blog was on rank 154 of the UK general blog charts, while the top-ranked German environmental blog was on rank 567 in the general ranking.

When looking at the top 20 general blog ranking, it is striking that the topics in the German ranking are much more diverse than the UK top blogs, which cover a very limited range of topics, as the graphs below clearly illustrate.

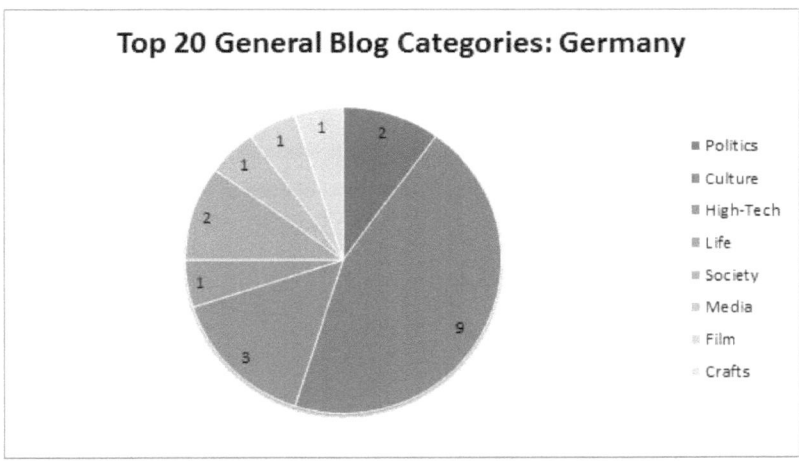

Figure 6: Top 20 General Blog Categories Germany

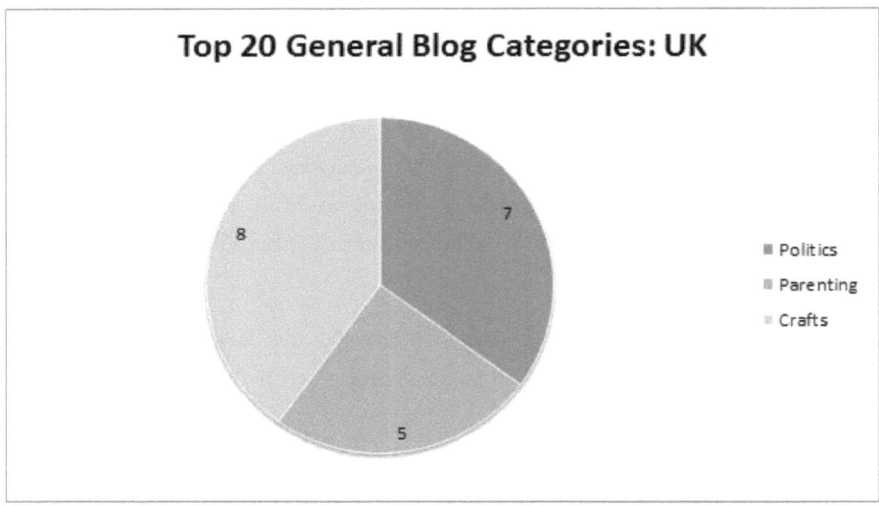

Figure 7: Top 20 General Blog Categories UK

The implications of the environmental blogosphere being of little importance in the blogosphere as a whole as well as the effects of the strong fragmentation of topics of German blogs will be addressed in the following chapter.

4.9. SUMMARY OF FINDINGS

The results of the analysis can be summarised as:

- The most popular blog category for German blogs was "Sustainable Lifestyle", while for the UK blogs it was "Parliamentary & Public Debates".
- UK environmental blogs had slightly longer entries on average
- UK blog readers commented more than the readers of the German sample
- German blogs contained more links to external sources than UK blogs
- For both countries, there were 40% of multi-authored blogs
- 60% of UK blogs were non-personal compared to 40% of German blogs
- The word "I" was used much more on UK blogs than on German blogs
- The relative importance of the environmental blogosphere seems low in both countries, but especially so in Germany

4.10. CONCLUSION

When looked at on their own, most of the different aspects that have been analysed here do not show significant differences between German and UK environmental blogs at first glance. However, combined with each other it is possible to draw significant conclusions about the environmental blogospheres in the two countries and these can be used to draw conclusions about a more holistic picture of the environmental movement and society in general in those two European countries.

The following chapter will support and interpret the findings with the help of secondary data and will link back to the literature review.

5. Discussion and Synthesis of the Findings

The aim of this chapter is to analyse and synthesise the findings of the primary research presented in the previous chapter. They will be analysed within the context of the findings from the literature review and the following chapter will consequently draw conclusions and provide recommendations for future research.

5.1. ANALYSIS OF BLOG STRUCTURES

This first part of the discussion will compare the structural features of the German and UK environmental blogospheres in terms of thematic categories, length of entries, number of comments, number of links, number of authors and finally purpose of the blog.

5.1.1. Categories

One of the central differences of German and UK environmental blogs appears to be their thematic focus. While the central topic on German environmental blogs was sustainable lifestyle, UK blogs tended to focus mostly on reporting about and commenting on parliamentary and other public debates about environmental issues. A total of four main categories for blog topics was identified: Parliamentary and Public Debates, Activism, Sustainable Lifestyle as well as Renewable Energy / Climate Change. Each will be discussed in detail below.

5.1.1.1. Parliamentary and Public Debates

The category "parliamentary and public debates" deals with environmental issues discussed in parliament or otherwise publicly via the mass media. This category contains blogs that report about and comment on such debates.

While only 15% of German blogs deal with parliamentary and other public debates, this number was significantly higher for UK blogs (40%). In fact, this was the major topic on UK environmental blogs.

For Germany, these results stand in contrast to what was concluded in the literature review. According to the findings there, the majority of blogs in Germany covers political issues. This seems not to be true for the environmental blogosphere, which puts sustainable lifestyle in the centre of coverage. This could be seen as a confirmation for what the media scholar Neuberger (Deutschlandfunk, 2011, see section 2.2.6.) suspects; the German press might be good enough to make a strong "counterweight" in the shape of blogs, like it exists for example in the United States, unnecessary. If this supposition is seen in connection with the fact that environmental issues rank relatively high in German public policy, not least because the Green Party is so powerful in Germany, society might be rather satisfied with how environmental issues are handled and reported on and thus there might be comparatively little need for exhaustive debates on blogs.

Another possible explanation could also be derived from the literature review. Neuberger (Deutschlandfunk, 2011) suggests that the German political blogger community is rather elitist, most of those bloggers might thus not strive to reach the top of blog rankings, which could explain why only few blogs of this kind were amongst the top-ranked environmental blogs. This theory could also be supported by the previously mentioned debate about blogs and the public sphere (see section 2.2.3.), in which it is argued that not all bloggers intend to be part of the public sphere, but are merely looking for a way to communicate with friends, family or colleagues (Schönberger, 2008). The bloggers from the German parliamentary and public debate category might thus not be interested to be among the top-ranked environmental blogs.

It could also be the combination of the elitist blog community and the absence of reasons to blog about environmental politics that explains the small percentage of parliamentary and public debate environmental blogs in Germany.

Concerning the share of parliamentary and public debate blogs among the UK sample, section 4.8. demonstrated that politics is one of the main themes in the UK blogosphere as a whole. This is reflected in the results for the environmental blogosphere, 40% of the blogs dealing with parliamentary and public debates and 30% dealing with activism, which is closely related to parliamentary and public debates. However, this raises the question why political discussions on environmental issues are such a popular topic in the UK. The literature review (chapter 2) suggested that in Germany, the political exclusion of environmental issues triggered an oppositional counter-culture during the late 1960's and the 1970's, while this did not happen in the UK. It is possible that this development was deferred in the UK and only develops now that activists have a powerful communication channel, the internet, at their disposal. This counter-culture could be further empowered by the relatively big support that the Green Party has among the population, which however does not lead to corresponding parliamentary representation. This could imply that things are exactly opposite of how they are in Germany: UK bloggers might feel that there is a need for a counterweight to the press and a sort of "extraparliamentary opposition" which combats the partial exclusion of environmental issues from politics. Future research could test this hypothesis, for example by interviewing bloggers.

5.1.1.2. Activism

The category "activism", which contains blogs that appeal to their readers to become active and support causes and movements, was assigned to only 10% of the German environmental blogs, but 30% of the UK blogs. In both samples the international NGO Greenpeace was found among the top five.

Several possible explanations exist for the difference in quantity of activism blogs. The low number of German activism blogs could be traced back to a not so mature blogosphere in Germany (see section 2.2.6. of the literature review). Most activism blogs found in both samples were maintained by NGOs and it is therefore possible that members of NGOs in Germany have either not yet realised the value of blogging or they might not be able to promote their blogs adequately to reach the top ranks of the Wikio ranking.

The other theory is again rooted in the previously illustrated supposition that environmental issues play a relatively important role in German politics and that therefore less activism is needed in the perception of the German society.

The UK NGOs however seem to be more skilled in capturing their audiences and appear on the top ranks of the environmental blogosphere. This is supported by the finding that 60% of the UK environmental blogs had non-personal purposes; compared to only 40% on the German side (see also section 4.6.).

Additionally, as already seen, environmental politics play a much bigger role in the UK blogosphere than in the German one and activism is closely related to the category parliamentary and public debates, as activism usually evolves from dissatisfaction with political activities. One example is the activism blog Suitably Despairing (http://suitablydespairing.blogspot.com/), which uses its blog to engage with and inform its audiences about nuisances such as oil spills that can often be traced back to mistakes in politics and legislation.

If the percentages for the categories parliamentary and public debates and activism were to be added up, this would result in 25% for Germany and 70% for the UK. This combined category that is mostly politically-driven thus accounts for one quarter of the German environmental blogosphere, but almost three quarters of the UK environmental blogosphere. This indicates that the UK blog readers are much more politicised than the German ones, which again stands in contrast to the fact that researchers believe that politics is the central theme of German blogs. Possibly, research about blog themes in Germany has not been intensive enough yet to really validate this statement. The environmental blogosphere is a counterexample of it and future research should be conducted to obtain a better overview of blog themes in Germany (see also chapter 6.2.).

5.1.1.3. Sustainable Lifestyle

The major theme of the German sample was sustainable lifestyle (60%), but this segment was only half as large in the UK sample (30%). Sustainable lifestyle blogs inform the readers about ways to lead a sustainable life, for example by eating biologically produced food, by reducing emissions released by buildings or by producing renewable energy at home using solar panels.

While environmental blogs, as seen in the previous sections, are dominated by political themes in the UK, the role of the individual in making human life sustainable for the planet is the central topic in Germany.

Could cultural factors be responsible for this? Geert Hofstede, a Dutch scholar specialised in researching cultural differences across the world, developed a model that makes it possible to compare different cultures: The Five Dimensions of Culture. These include the Power Distance Index (PDI), Individualism (IDV), Masculinity (MAS), Uncertainty Avoidance Index (UAI) and Long-Term Orientation (LTO) (Hofstede, 2001).

For the considerations about sustainable lifestyle, the most interesting dimension is Individuality, which Hofstede defines as the extent to which individuals are connected to groups. That refers to the question whether everyone is supposed to take care of himself or whether everyone works for the welfare of a group. Hofstede points out that "group" does not necessarily refer to nations, but could also refer to families, school classes and the like (Hofstede, 2001).

As the graph below (Hofstede, 2011) shows, the UK indeed scores very high for Individualism (IDV); 89 out of 100 points to be precise. Germany reaches a score of 67 out of 100.

The 5D Model of professor Geert Hofstede

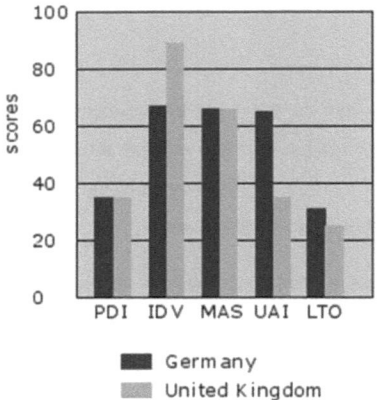

Figure 8: The 5D Model of professor Geert Hofstede

These results point towards a (partially) culturally motivated difference between the German and the UK interest in sustainability for the welfare of humanity. According to Hofstede's figures, the UK culture is more individualistic, meaning in this case that people might be more interested in having a "good life" as an individual without paying too much attention to how sustainable their daily behaviour is (e.g. dealing with waste, food or energy) and how this affects other people and future generations. For Germany, the individuality score was much lower, which in this context can imply that people attempt to handle issues of sustainability more responsibly with an eye on other people and future generations.

According to the current Target Group Index (TGI) market research (TGI Europa, 2011), which compares the willingness to act in an environmentally friendly way across several European countries, the UK achieved the lowest score with 38% willing to restrict their lifestyle in favour of the environment. Germany achieved a slightly higher score of 41%. The TGI report also mentions that the awareness for environmental issues is very high in Germany and 98% of Germans said to concern themselves with environmental issues, but as the previous score for willingness to act accordingly shows, there is a great discrepancy between considering the environment and acting in its favour. This could explain why there are many top-ranked blogs with sustainable lifestyle themes in Germany. The high ranking shows that readers are concerned about sustainability and "push" sustainability issues to the top of the environmental blogosphere. Also, bloggers probably realise the discrepancy between thinking and acting and thus start to blog about sustainable issues in order to motivate readers to act in a sustainable way.

5.1.1.4. Renewable Energy / Climate Change

The fourth category established was "renewable energy / climate change", which mostly contains blogs that deal with the more scientific aspect of energy and climate change, as opposed to the category sustainable lifestyle, which takes a more personal approach. 25% of the German sample falls under this category, while for the UK sample it is 15%.

In Germany, renewable energy is omnipresent. Current statistics reveal that already 22.4% of energy produced comes from renewable sources, while in the UK energy production from renewable sources accounts for only 2.9% (Destatis/Eurostat, 2011). Besides, the German government decided to shut down all nuclear power plants within the next couple of years which forces the economy to rethink and challenges science to come up with sustainable energy solutions as soon as possible. It is thus not surprising that renewable energy is on the agenda of German environmental bloggers.

But even though the UK produces only very small amounts of renewable energy compared to Germany, it is an important topic in the UK environmental blogosphere. Similar to the previously discussed categories, it is possible that in this case again bloggers attempt to draw attention to this issue because they feel that it is being neglected by politics (see also: deferred counter-culture, section 5.1.1.). As demonstrated in the literature review, the green sister parties exert little political power and lobbying for environmental interests is not very successful, either. Therefore it is likely that the "lobby" shifts to the blogosphere in order to generate awareness among blog readers and eventually create pressure for the government to act. It could be concluded therefore, that here the internet is deliberately used as a public sphere (see also section 2.2.3.) in order to fuel debates and ultimately to influence political action.

5.1.1.5. Summary of Blog Category Analysis

From the analysis of blog categories, the main conclusions that can be drawn include that the UK's environmental blogosphere is more politicised than the German one, but that in turn German blogs concentrate on matters of sustainable lifestyle, which might have cultural reasons.

5.1.2. Length of entries

The length of blog entries, that is the number of words per entry, can shed light on the function or purpose a blog fulfils. As shown in the analysis chapter, the UK blog entries tended to be slightly longer than the German ones, with UK entries having 448 words compared to 371 words for German entries. Earlier research indicated that average entries only had 210.4 words (Herring et al., 2004a).

For the UK blogs in the sample, the number of words was thus more than twice as high and also the German sample showed a significantly higher number of words per entry than previous research suggested. The longest entry that Herring et al. found in their study had 1,262 words, which comes quite close to the longest entry in the German sample, which had 1,523 words. However, in the UK sample there were five entries which had more than 2,000 words, the longest entry having 3,829 words.

It is unclear, why the German and UK blogs sampled for this study have significantly longer entries on average than Herring's sample. It could point towards a tendency either in the area of environmental topics or in the blogosphere as a whole for the texts to become longer over time. After all, Herring's study dates back to 2004 and the blogosphere has undergone continuous development since. Another reason for the entries to be comparatively long might be the fact that the blogs sampled for this study are the top blogs in their category and so the bloggers might invest more time in blogging than the random bloggers who have been in Herring's sample. Possibly, the top environmental bloggers feel more committed to their audience and attempt to deliver high quality entries of a certain length.

The differences between German and UK environmental blogs however were rather small, with UK entries having only 77 more words on average, which equals only few sentences. Consequently, it can be said that in terms of entry length, there are no significant differences between the two countries' environmental blogospheres. As it could be seen previously, the topics of the individual blogs are more revealing and it will be argued further later in this chapter that the differences are not rooted so much in structural elements of the blogs, but more in the contents.

5.1.3. Comments

It is the goal of many bloggers to engage with their readers via the comment function, as seen in the literature review. A big number of comments can point towards a large and engaged readership. The research revealed that UK blogs received more comments on average and had more entries which had comments at all. This indicates that UK environmental blogs have a larger readership and/or more engaged readers. This chapter will also argue later that the environmental blogosphere is more popular in the UK than in Germany, which is most probably the reason for a bigger readership and consequently also for more comments.

In a previously conducted study in which Herring et al. (2004a) randomly sampled 203 blogs in English language, they found out that entries had only 0.3 comments on average, the majority of entries thus did not have any comments at all. For the German and UK environmental blogs, this did not hold completely true. As seen in the previous chapter, 50.0% of UK blog entries and 60.75% of German blog entries did not receive any comments, yet the average and median was 4.24/1.28 for the UK entries and 2.53/1.13 for German entries. The median had been calculated because some outliers significantly influenced the average of the UK sample.

There are several possible explanations for the discrepancy with Herring's study. First, Herring's study was conducted in 2004 and it can be assumed that by now (summer 2011), as presented in the literature review, the blogosphere has tremendously increased in size and therefore the number of readers to leave comments has also increased. Secondly, Herring's sample was randomly selected while for this study only top-ranked blogs were sampled, which, due to the higher number of readers, makes it comprehensible that highly-ranked blogs receive more comments. Finally, the topics discussed in the top-ranked environmental blogs are often controversial and previous research revealed that controversial and insightful blog entries tend to receive more comments than others (Krishnamurthy, 2002).

When taking these three factors into account, it seems quite probable that more prominent blogospheres, such as the political blogosphere would even receive significantly more comments. So, although the number of comments in the German and UK top environmental blogs was higher than the numbers that Herring et al. found, it can still be assumed that the environmental blogosphere in both countries is rather small compared to other blogospheres. This point will be further enforced later in this chapter.

5.1.4. Links

Links are agreed to be a central feature of blogging. The level of interconnectedness can provide clues about to what degree a blog stands in the centre of the blogosphere (or a particular part of it). Also, rankings such as the Wikio ranking that was used for this study, determine the rank of a site, among other factors, by counting how many links lead to a site.

It was found that German blogs entries contain more links than UK ones on average. Herring et al. (2004, cited in Pedersen and Macafee, 2007a) previously found that only 31.8% of the entries in their sample contained any links at all. This study however finds that 86.0% of German entries and 86.25% of UK entries contained links. Similarly to the number of comments discussed in the previous section, this divergence could be explained by the fact that Herring's study dates back to 2004 when the blogosphere was still less developed than it is now. Additionally, the sample of this study contains only top-ranked blogs which might cause the bloggers to feel an obligation to provide evidence for their claims by linking to external sources. And, since the internet as a whole is growing, there are of course more sources to be linked to which might have not been there back in 2004 when Herring et al. conducted their research.

But even though almost all entries in both the UK and the German environmental blogs contained links, it could be seen that German blogs provided more links per entry on average. As it will be argued later in this chapter, it seems that the UK blogs are more subjective than the German ones. Expressing own opinions decreases the necessity to provide evidence for claims, which could explain the smaller number of links in the UK sample. Since own opinions tend to be more controversial than claims that can be proven with facts, this could also explain the higher number of comments on UK blogs.

However, the lower number of links on UK environmental blogs also raises the question whether the UK blogosphere is really further developed than the German blogosphere in all aspects, as previous research presented in the literature review suggests. The literature review further showed that links and the interconnectedness which results from linking is a central attribute of the blogosphere. From this it can be concluded that blogging in Germany is starting to catch up, at least in the field of environmental blogs and interconnectedness. Further research should be conducted in order to find out whether the findings of this study mirror the entire German blogosphere.

5.1.5. Authors

Blogs can have more than one author. This section will speculate about the effects and purposes of multi-authored blogs.

When it comes to distinguishing single- and multi-authored blogs, the differences between UK and German environmental blogs seem to be negligible. 40% of both samples were multi-authored blogs. Although the sample size of this study was too small for statistic justifications, it is striking that there is a big deviance with earlier research. Again, a comparison is made with research conducted by Herring, whose work is very influential in blog research. In a longitudinal blog analysis performed in the course of 2003 and 2004 with a total of 457 randomly selected blogs, Herring et al. (2007a) found that there were 8.8% of multiple-authored blogs in early 2003 and 11.0% in early 2004. Even though Herring's findings show a slight upward trend, it is surprising that in 2011, for German and UK environmental blogs, 40% of multi-authored blogs were found. A possible reason for this was assumed to be the fact that many blogs in the samples belonged to NGOs or other types of organizations (see following section) which might have multiple employees or members to take care of the organizational blog. However, this assumption proved wrong as calculations by the author showed that there is no relationship between the number of blog authors and the blog purpose.

Possibly, considering that the sampled blogs are highly ranked, being a group of authors makes it easier to maintain a certain quality standard for blog entries thanks to shared workload and to keep the blog updated regularly. The scope of this study is too small to test this hypothesis, but further research could provide clarity on this matter.

5.1.6. Blog Purpose

The sampled blogs have also been analysed according to their purpose. This refers to blogs being personal or being used by organizations such as companies or non-governmental organizations (NGOs) or public figures such as politicians for their respective goals. The fact that 40% of the German blogs and 60% of the UK blogs had non-personal purposes seems to confirm that commercially used blogs are on the rise.

Researchers have already discovered that corporate blogging is increasingly used as a relationship management tool which is already widely used in the US (Cho and Huh, 2010). Apparently also organizations in the UK and, to a smaller extent, Germany have discovered the benefits of blogs for managing relationships with stakeholders. Benefits include for example being able to communicate with stakeholders in a conversational tone and giving a "human face" to an organization (Kelleher and Miller, 2006).

If it is still the case that Germany is lagging behind other countries when it comes to blogging, as it has been concluded in previous sections, this could explain why the number of non-personal blogs in the top ranks of the environmental blogosphere is smaller in Germany than in the UK. It will be argued later in this chapter that many German environmental activists and NGOs might not yet have the skills to engage their audiences on blogs. Furthermore, in the UK sample some politicians were present while in the German sample there were none. Blogging for PR or otherwise non-personal purposes thus seems to be less developed in Germany even though the benefits are obvious.

Another observation that was striking for both countries was that many non-personal blogs were not identifiable as such at first glance. Often, it could only be found out when reading the "about" page or some small print. Possible reasons why organizations or groups may wish to obscure commercial or non-personal interests include being able to manipulate readers' opinions more subtly or to be more credible.

5.1.7. Summary from the Analysis of Blog Structures

Despite of discrepancies with previous blog research (especially Herring et al., 2007a), suggesting that a general advancement of the blogosphere has taken place since 2004, the structural differences of German and UK blogs were not very significant, for most parts. There is evidence that the German blogosphere is still slightly less developed than the UK one, with one exception being its interconnectedness through links. Judging by the number of comments, it seems that the environmental blogosphere in both countries is rather small.

The most important aspect that illustrates the differences between the two blogospheres is the dissimilar distribution of categories. While UK environmental blogs are clearly more politically focused, German environmental blogs tend to cover issues on sustainable lifestyle. As it will be shown in the next section, the most striking and significant differences can be found in the contents of the blog entries.

5.2. Miscellaneous Factors

Next to the structural features of the two blogospheres, it has also been looked at opinions uttered by bloggers, as well as the relative importance of the blogospheres in Germany and the UK. The results will be discussed in the following sections.

5.2.1. Opinions in the Blogosphere

During data collection and analysis, a remarkable discovery was made: UK environmental bloggers seem to talk about themselves and their opinion much more frequently than their German counterparts. This was found out by counting the number of "I"'s in both samples. While on German environmental blogs "I" is used 5.8 times per 1,000 words on average, it is used 9.03 times on their UK counterparts, thus suggesting that UK bloggers express their opinions more strongly than German ones.

Additional evidence for this hypothesis can be gained from the average number of links that has been mentioned previously. German blogs tend to link to more external sources for background information and proof, while personal views play a bigger role on UK blogs. Also the slightly higher number of comments could be added as evidence for this hypothesis. Giving personal views on topics while at the same time providing fewer proves in the shape of links for those views could be the reason for people to start a discussion and give their own opinions on the topic.

But what are the reasons for UK bloggers to express their opinions more strongly? This section provides possible explanations for the phenomenon.

A manifest explanation for the UK's more egocentric writing style could be that it is rooted in the British culture. As introduced previously in this chapter, the Dutch scholar Hofstede (2001) developed the model of the Five Dimensions of Culture. For the considerations about the UK bloggers focusing more on their own opinion, the Individuality Index will be considered again. To remind the reader, individuality refers to the importance of an individual within a group. Germany scored 67/100 and the UK scored 89/100, the UK culture thus being more individualistic than German one.

Since individuality is distinct in the UK, it stands to reason that writers talk about themselves more frequently, which was in this case measured by counting the number of "I"'s per 1,000 words of text. German bloggers used the German equivalent for "I" significantly less, which points towards a less individualistic culture, which is also confirmed by Hofstede's figures.

Could it be possible that there are linguistic reasons as well? It seems that linguistic research comparing German and English language blogs is either very scarce or non-existent. However, previous research on academic writing styles comparing German and English native speakers suggests that Germans have a preference for using impersonal and passive sentence constructions (Clyne, 1991), thus effectively avoiding the use of the personal pronoun "I". It is not clear whether this applies to more informal writing, such as in blogs, too. However, the possibility that German environmental bloggers express their opinions just as much as UK bloggers, but do so more subtly by using impersonal and passive sentence structures, should not be eliminated. Future research could shed light on this question.

The question whether UK environmental bloggers indeed express their opinions more strongly could thus not be entirely clarified. The argument of cultural differences has however been given more weight, as the evidence concerning linguistics is not tailored to blog writing and it is therefore not clear whether German writers also use more passive and impersonal sentence structures when writing for blogs. For now, it will therefore be assumed that the cultural theory is more likely until further research will be able to refute it.

5.2.2. Relative Importance of the Environmental Blogosphere

How important are environmental blogs for the blogosphere as a whole? The analysis revealed that the top-ranked UK environmental blog was on rank 154 of the UK blogosphere as a whole, while the best German environmental blog could be found only on rank 567 of the German general ranking. The analysis also showed that in the general rankings the variety of topics was much bigger in the German blogosphere than in the UK blogosphere.

For Germany, this fragmentation of the general blogosphere stands in contrast to what researchers believe to be the central topic on German blogs, namely politics. It might be that the blogosphere is changing too quickly for researchers and publications in academic journals to keep pace with the developments. The other option is that Wikio's ranking algorithm is different from what researchers usually do to research blogs.

Be that as it may, a plausible explanation for why the UK top environmental blog scores relatively high in the general ranking compared to its German counterpart is that it covers mostly political issues (from the categories parliamentary and public debates and activism), which, according to the Wikio ranking, play an important role in the UK blogosphere. While the blogosphere in general covers all political streams, the environmental blogosphere naturally has a focus on green politics and how politics deal with environmental questions.

The fact that the German environmental blogosphere seems to be of little importance for the general blogosphere is surprising, given that environmental issues are so present in the public sphere (see chapter 2.3.3.). When looking at the ranking history of the German top-ranked environmental blog it becomes visible that in September 2009 the blog was on rank 130 of the general blogosphere, thus on a similar position as the UK top-ranked environmental blog is now. Consequently, something must have happened since 2009 that moved the environmental blogs so far behind. A reasonable explanation is the development of the German blogosphere. As illustrated previously, blogging seems to be lagging behind in Germany, compared to the UK or the US. This study also found evidence though that blogs have further developed compared to a 2004 study of blog structures by Herring et al. (2007a). This progress might have led to a comparatively late "professionalization" of the German blogosphere which brought the more skilled bloggers to the top ranks, those who aptly manage to attract big audiences and keep them engaged. This is supported by the findings from the literature review, suggesting that the declining growth rate of the blogosphere is a sign that only "serious" and thus more professional bloggers remain in the long run.

As also stated previously, the environmental blogosphere is a niche blogosphere and the only factor that keeps the UK environmental blogs relatively high in the ranking is the fact that predominantly political issues are covered, which depict one of the major fields of interest of UK blog users. The major category of German environmental blogs (sustainable lifestyle) is not one of the dominant topics among German blogs in general though and the proportion of bloggers with the skills to effectively promote their blog is therefore likely to be small compared to bloggers blogging about more popular topics. This could explain why the environmental blogs are so far behind other blog types and why the relative importance of environmental blogs has decreased in recent years in Germany.

5.2.3. Summary of Miscellaneous Findings

The second part of the primary research found that UK environmental bloggers express their own opinions to a bigger extent than the German ones, which manifests itself in the use of the personal pronoun "I". It is likely that the higher degree of individuality in the British culture is responsible for this.

Next to that, it was concluded that the environmental blogosphere plays a relatively bigger role for the whole blogosphere in the UK than in Germany. The cause for this is seen in the fact that UK environmental blogs tend to cover political issues, which generally rank high in the UK blogosphere. Additionally, it was suspected that German environmental bloggers are less skilled than the average blogger and so might not be able to capture large audiences, even though environmentalism is a popular topic in German public debate.

The following chapter will present the central conclusions gained from the findings discussed above. It will also provide recommendations for further research, as well as limitations of the study.

6. Conclusions

This final chapter of the research paper will conclude the findings discussed in the previous chapter and summarise concisely what the results are for each of the research objectives. For the convenience of the reader, the research aim and objectives are repeated once again:

Research aim:

To advance an understanding of the distinctive characteristics of the German as well as the UK environmental blogosphere in terms of structure and content

Research objectives:

1. Identify how environmental movements have developed in Germany and the UK and assess their current state
2. Evaluate critically relevant knowledge on central features and characteristics of blogs in general, as well as blogs in Germany and the UK in particular
3. Explore and compare features of the German and the UK environmental blogosphere in terms of structure and content
4. Formulate an accurate snapshot of the current state of the German and UK environmental blogosphere and illustrate the implications of the findings

This chapter will now revisit each objective, summarise the findings presented in the previous chapter and offer conclusions and implications. Afterwards, recommendations for further research, as well as limitations of the study will round up the research paper.

6.1. RESEARCH OBJECTIVES: SUMMARY OF FINDINGS AND CONCLUSIONS

6.1.1. Objective 1: Environmental Movements in Germany and the UK

The literature review showed that the political influence of environmental movements (and its' "child", the Green Party) is bigger in Germany than in the UK. Nevertheless, primary research conducted within the scope of this study suggests that blogging significantly strengthens the UK environmental movement, making room for extensive (political) blog coverage, which, compared to the German environmental blogs, is quite highly ranked in the UK hierarchy of blogs as a whole. German (green) political forces on the other hand, seem to not have realised the potential of blogging or to be unable to promote their blogs successfully. Also the fact that in Germany blogging is perhaps not considered a necessary counterweight to the press is suspected to play a role here.

6.1.2. Objective 2: Previous Research on Blogging

The literature review suggested that Germany is lagging behind when it comes to blogging. This study produced evidence that this is still the case, however, it was also demonstrated that previous results from content analysis are not up to date anymore, at least not concerning the environmental blogospheres of the two countries.

The comparison between literature, which is naturally not entirely up to date due to the lengthy process of publishing, and primary research on structural features of blogs shows that the blogosphere along with the world-wide-web as a whole is changing rapidly and on a constant basis. There were discrepancies between earlier research and this research, for example in the average length of blog entries, the average number of comments, the percentage of entries that contain links, and the proportion of multi-authored blogs. These discrepancies call for a bigger number of longitudinal blog studies, which, judging from past blog developments might be able to predict the future of blogging to a certain degree. This would also serve the environmental blogosphere and the environmental movement in particular, because it could maximise its efforts to combat for a sustainable future.

Also, previously conducted research suggesting that the majority of German blogs covers politics seems to be outdated. Research into the environmental blogosphere revealed that politics play a minor role in this particular context and superficial research conducted within the scope of this study into the general blogosphere showed that the top ranks of the German blogosphere are occupied by a wide variety of themes.

6.1.3. Objective 3: Features of the German and UK Environmental Blogosphere

Although structure-wise there were big differences with previous research (especially with Herring et al., 2007a) which points towards a general progress of the blogosphere since 2004, the structural differences of German and UK blogs were mostly rather small. The major factors of importance that were discovered, were the more political orientation of UK blogs and a confirmation that the German blogosphere seems to be slightly lagging behind in development compared to the UK blogosphere.

Another striking and significant difference can be found in the contents of the blog entries. The main result here was that, probably caused by cultural differences, UK environmental bloggers express their opinions more strongly than German environmental bloggers, using the personal pronoun "I".

The research results also show that blogging does not seem to be very popular among German environmentalists. The relative importance of the German environmental blogosphere in the total blogosphere significantly decreased, which was substantiated by the professionalization of blogging in Germany, which environmental bloggers do not appear to keep up with, resulting in the environmental blogosphere losing popularity while other thematic blogospheres managed to capture more readers. In the UK, the relative importance of the environmental blogosphere is higher than in Germany, although it is certainly not one of the most significant ones. The reasons why the UK environmental blogosphere could "defend" its position in the general ranking was attributed to the fact that a big proportion of UK environmental blogs covers political issues, which are generally very popular in the UK blogosphere.

In conclusion it can be said that UK environmental blogs are generally more professional than German ones in terms of attracting readers and gaining popularity in the general blogosphere. However, it can also be said that UK environmental blogs are more focused on advancing opinions while the German ones have a rather objective approach, passing on news and providing information to the readers. The implications of this will be discussed in the following section.

6.1.4. Objective 4: Combining the Findings to Provide an Accurate Snapshot of the German and UK Environmental Blogospheres and Illustrating the Implications

The previous sections have provided conclusions gained from the research. This section will now illustrate the implications of these conclusions for the environmental movements in Germany and the UK as well as for blogging and the blogosphere. There will also be recommendations for environmental bloggers. The next section will provide recommendations for further research, as not all results discovered during research could be clarified within the scope of this study.

The power of bloggers, although not comparable to the US bloggers' power, seems to be rather high in the UK. This implies that blogging has the potential for the UK environmental movements to gain more power and ultimately pressure politics to act more in the interest of the environment. For the environmental movement and the possibly deferred development of an oppositional counter-culture protesting against the vast exclusion of environmental issues from the political agenda, this is the chance to gain strength and help get the ball rolling.

Also, the German environmental movement, which is already comparatively strong, could be further strengthened, provided the power of blogging is recognised and it is learned how to draw attention to the environmental blogs. However, blogging seems to be less significant in Germany than in the UK, which implies that the benefits gained from blogging are likely to be smaller in Germany than in the UK.

For blogging in general, the results of this study revealed the need for more intensive blog research, which goes for country-specific research as well as for the type of research; the need for more longitudinal blog studies has been demonstrated. Intensified research on blogs will also benefit other academic disciplines, such as cultural research and linguistics. The significance of blogging in the USA has already been widely recognised and if similar developments are to take place in Europe and other parts of the world, research that has been conducted in advance can have a positive impact and to a certain extent influence the developments. Specific recommendations for further research are provided later in this chapter.

6.1.5. Recommendations to Environmental Bloggers

The biggest problem for the environmental bloggers, especially the German ones, seems to be the lack of attention and a small readership. The author recommends using social media such as Facebook, Google+ and Twitter in order to engage audiences more intensively and to find new readers.

Besides, countless online and offline guidebooks exist which provide tips for creating successful blogs. The author believes that it would be beneficial for the environmental blogs to try and establish a network with other environmental blogs as well as with other (mainstream) media, as increased media coverage of the issues presented on the environmental blogs will create more public awareness and eventually create pressure for politics to act. A network of interlinked environmental blogs will also strengthen the role of the environmental blogosphere in the blogosphere as a whole and improve search engine ranks, which can consequently increase the number of blog readers.

6.2. RECOMMENDATIONS FOR FURTHER RESEARCH

The analysis and discussion of the research findings has produced a variety of useful results, but it has also uncovered some areas that it cannot sufficiently illuminate as they go beyond the scope of this study. Therefore, this section will provide recommendations for further research.

6.2.1. Longitudinal Blog Studies

As stated previously, this piece of research can be regarded as a snapshot of the current situation of the environmental blogosphere in Germany and the UK and it could become part of a longitudinal analysis of German and UK (environmental) blogs. It was paid attention to this in terms of research design and the replicability of the study has been maximised as much as possible, as explained in chapter 3. As the conclusions of this study illustrated, the blogosphere seems to have changed significantly compared to a 2004 study by Herring et al. which demonstrates the need for longitudinal blog analyses.

6.2.2. State of the German Blogosphere

The literature review suggested that politics is the main topic of the German blogosphere, but neither the in-depth analysis of environmental blogs nor the general top 20 ranking by Wikio confirmed this. Further quantitative research should be conducted to make a contribution to the categorisation of the German blogosphere so that it can be looked at in a more differentiated manner.

Additionally, the results of the primary research indicated that, at least in terms of interconnectedness, the German environmental blogosphere is further developed than the UK one. Further research should be conducted in order to find out whether this is true for the entire German blogosphere.

6.2.3. Public Figures in the German Blogosphere

The comparison between German and UK environmental blogs revealed that among the UK sample there were "public figures" such as MPs and journalists while there were none in the German sample. Further research could investigate the causes for this. It might have to do with the German blogosphere being less developed or German public figures might not have the skills to attract large audiences to their blogs.

6.2.4. Correlation of Number of Authors and Rank of a Blog

During the discussion of findings, the fact that many of the top-ranked blogs were maintained by multiple authors was speculated about. Possible reasons could be that multiple authors find it easier to update the blog regularly and to provide different angles of looking at topics. It is also possible that multi-authored blogs are popular because they maintain a high quality standard thanks to peer reviewing. Multiple authors might also be more committed to the blog as part of a team. However, these are only speculations and further research could reveal the truth about the correlation between the number of authors and blog rank, also for other blogospheres.

6.2.5. Linguistics on Blogs

Although there has been some research about language use on the internet, science is still lacking a comparative study of German and Anglophone language on the internet or on blogs in particular. This could help to clarify the question whether the augmented use of the personal pronoun "I" in the UK sample is rooted in linguistics or indeed culture, as suspected in this study.

6.2.6. Deferred Environmental Movement in the UK

In the previous chapter it was presumed that the oppositional counter-culture or extraparliamentary opposition, which had developed in Germany during the 1960's and 1970's due to exclusion of environmental topics by the government, might have been deferred in the UK and possibly only develops now that the UK environmentalists have found a powerful ally in the shape of the internet. This assumption should be backed up by correspondent in-depth research.

6.2.7. Scotland's Role in Environmental Blogging

A striking fact discovered was that many of the top-ranked UK environmental blogs specifically dealt with Scotland. Although some attempts were made to figure out the reasons for this, no satisfactory answer could be found. Thus, it seems that there are complex reasons for it, which requires further research, ideally by UK nationals or other specialists, who perhaps have a better understanding of domestic issues than the author of this study, who only spent a few months in the UK.

6.3. Contribution to Knowledge

Although both the environmental movements and the blogosphere have been researched previously, this study is unique in combining the knowledge gained from the two disciplines as well as conducting primary research on the environmental blogosphere of two countries. Also the comparative approach, although it has been used in comparing environmental movements as well as blogospheres of different countries, is unique in the context of the environmental blogosphere. Despite the new linking of already existent knowledge combined with primary research, this study has made use of an established and academically sound research design containing well-known research methods in the form of content analysis and grounded theory.

The results of this study can be seen as basic and exploratory research of a yet widely unknown blogosphere – the environmental blogosphere. The results showed that there were meanderings from general previous blog research as well as between the two countries. This study can therefore be regarded as the basis for further research, as also described in the previous section which provided a selection of topics that require further research.

Despite being basic, this research adds to the general knowledge about blogs and public concern about the environment. It can also be used by scholars of other academic disciplines, for example those dealing with cultural theory and linguistics and the research also offers new facts about Anglo-German differences in particular.

6.4. Limitations of the Study

Despite being carefully planned and executed, there are some limitations to this study, which are presented below.

The major limitation of the study is its relatively small sample. The top 20 blogs from the UK and Germany each were analysed. However, this was found necessary because beyond the top 20, the blogs showed only little activity and many were abandoned which would have resulted in useless findings. Therefore, within the 20 sampled blogs 400 entries have been analysed in order to deliver enough data for reliable statistical analysis.

Also, considering that this was exploratory research into the largely unknown environmental blogosphere the time available for research has been rather short and the author worked on her own so that many questions remained unanswered, as the long list of recommendations for further research demonstrates. Nevertheless, this opens up research opportunities for other graduands or researchers.

Appendix I: References

ALLAN, G. 2003. A Critique of Using Grounded Theory as a Research Method. *The electronic Journal of Business Research Methods,* 2(1), pp. 1-10.

BBC NEWS. 2010. Election: Green Party gain first MP with Brighton win. 2011. [Online]. Available: http://news.bbc.co.uk/2/hi/uk_news/politics/election_2010/8666445.stm [Accessed 27 June 2011].

BLAWAT, K. 2011. Verkrampftes Verhältnis zur Natur. *sueddeutsche.de* [Online]. Available: http://www.sueddeutsche.de/wissen/kinder-verkrampftes-verhaeltnis-zur-natur-1.1130302 [Accessed 13 August 2011].

BLOOD, R. 2002. *The Weblog Handbook: Practical Advice on Creating and Maintaining Your Blog,* Cambridge: Perseus Publishing.

CASLON ANALYTICS. 2009. *Caslon Analytics blogging* [Online]. Available: http://www.caslon.com.au/weblogprofile1.htm#many [Accessed 16 June 2011].

CHENG, J. 2008. Blog growth slows; more bloggers are bringing home the bacon. *Ars Technica* [Online]. Available from: http://arstechnica.com/old/content/2008/09/blog-growth-slows-more-bloggers-are-bringing-home-the-bacon.ars [Accessed 06 September 2011].

CHO, S. & HUH, J. 2010. Content analysis of corporate blogs as a relationship management tool. *Corporate Communications: An International Journal,* 15(1), pp. 30-48.

CLAPP, B. W. 1994. *An Environmental History of Britain since the Industrial Revolution,* London: Longman.

CLASEN, J. (ed.) 1999. *Comparative Social Policy: Concepts, Theories and methods* Oxford: Blackwell.

CLYNE, M. 1991. The Sociocultural Dimension: The Dilemma of the German-speaking Scholar. *In:* SCHRÖDER, H. (ed.) *Subject-oriented Texts: Languages for Special Purposes and Text Theory.* Berlin: de Gruyter.

DALE, I. 2008. Mining for gold in the blogosphere. *British Journalism Review,* 19(4), pp. 31-36.

DALE, I. 2010a. *The guide to political blogging in the UK, 2010-11* London: Biteback.

DALE, I. 2010b. The Top 300 Political Blogs. *In:* DALE, I. (ed.) *Guide to Political Blogging in the UK.* London: Biteback.

DAYMON, C. 2002. *Qualitative Research Methods in Public Relations and Marketing Communications,* London: Routledge.

DEPARTMENT FOR ENVIRONMENT FOOD AND RURAL AFFAIRS. 2009. *2009 Survey of public attitudes and behaviours towards the environment.* [Online]. Available: http://www.defra.gov.uk/statistics/files/090923stats-release-pubatt.pdf [Accessed 08 April 2011].

DESTATIS/EUROSTAT. 2011. Erneuerbare Energien in Europa. [Online]. Available: http://www.destatis.de/jetspeed/portal/cms/Sites/destatis/Internet/DE/Content/Publikatio nen/Fachveroeffentlichungen/Internationales/FaltblattErneuerbareEnergien0040003119001, property=file.pdf [Accessed 23 August 2011].

DEUTSCHLANDFUNK. 2011. *Die Professionalisierung ist nicht so weit vorangeschritten wie in den USA [Digital Audio File]* [Online]. Germany: Deutschlandfunk. Available: http://www.dradio.de/dlf/sendungen/interview_dlf/1488369/ [Accessed 13 July 2011].

DOUGLAS, D. 2003. Grounded Theories of Management: A Methodological Review. *Management Research News,* 26(5), pp. 44-52.

DPA/AFP. 2011. Wulff unterzeichnet Atom-Ausstiegsgesetz. *Sueddeutsche.de* [Online]. Available: http://www.sueddeutsche.de/politik/politik-kompakt-an-israelisch-libanesischer-grenze-fallen-schuesse-1.1126610 [Accessed 13 August 2011].

DRYZEK, J. S., DOWNES, D., HUNOLD, C., SCHLOSBERG, D. & HERNES, H.-K. 2003. *Green States and Social Movements - Environmentalism in the United States, United Kingdom, Germany, and Norway,* Oxford: Oxford University Press.

ETLING, B., KELLY, J., FARIS, R. & PALFREY, J. 2010. Mapping the Arabic blogosphere: politics and dissent online. *New Media & Society,* 12(8), pp. 1225-1243.

GERHARDS, J. & SCHÄFER, M. S. 2010. Is the internet a better public sphere? Comparing old and new media in the USA and Germany. *New Media & Society,* 12(1), pp. 143-160.

GOODE, L. 2009. Social news, citizen journalism and democracy. *New Media & Society,* 11(8), pp. 1287-1305.

GREEN PARTY OF ENGLAND AND WALES. 2011. *About the Green Party* [Online]. Available: http://www.greenparty.org.uk/about.html [Accessed 27 June 2011].

HABERMAS, J. 1990. *Strukturwandel der Öffentlichkeit: Untersuchungen zu einer Kategorie der bürgerlichen Gesellschaft,* Frankfurt am Main: Suhrkamp.

HABERMAS, J. 2008. *Ach, Europa: Kleine politische Schriften XI,* Frankfurt am Main: Suhrkamp.

HARRIS, H. 2001. Content analysis of secondary data: A study of courage in managerial decision making. *Journal of Business Ethics,* 34(3), pp. 191 - 208.

HE, Y., CAROLI, F. & MANDL, T. (eds.) 2007. *The Chinese and the German Blogosphere: An Empirical and Comparative Analysis,* Munich: Oldenbourg

HEN/DPA/REUTERS/DAPD. 2011. Grüne erklimmen Rekordhoch, FDP stürzt ab. *Spiegel Online* [Online]. Available: http://www.spiegel.de/politik/deutschland/0,1518,755315,00.html [Accessed 07 April 2011].

HERRING, SCHEIDT, BONUS & WRIGHT. 2004a. Bridging the Gap: A Genre Analysis of Weblogs. *In:* Proceedings of 37th Hawaii International Conference on System Sciences, 2004 Hawaii.

HERRING, S., SCHEIDT, L. A., KOUPER I. & WRIGHT, E. 2004b. Women and children last: The discursive construction of Weblogs. *Into the blogosphere: Rhetoric, community and culture of Weblogs* [Online], 2011. Available: http://blog.lib.umn.edu/blogosphere/women_and_children.html [Accessed 16 June 2011].

HERRING, S., SCHEIDT, L. A., KOUPER I. & WRIGHT, E, 2007. A Longitudinal Content Analysis of Weblogs: 2003-2004. *In:* TREMAYNE, M. (ed.) *Blogging, Citizenship, and the Future of Media.* New York: Routledge.

HERRING, S. C., KOUPER, I., PAOLILLO, J. C., SCHEIDT, L. A., TYWORTH, M., WELSCH, P., WRIGHT, E. & YU, N. 2005a. Conversations in the Blogosphere: An Analysis "From the Bottom Up". *In:* Proceedings of 38th Hawaii International Conference on System Sciences, 2005 Hawaii.

HERRING, S. C., SCHEIDT, L. A., WRIGHT, E. & BONUS, S. 2005b. Weblogs as a bridging genre *Information Technology & People,* 18(2), pp. 142-171.

HOFSTEDE, G. 2001. *Culture's Consequences: Comparing Values, Behaviors, Institutions and Organizations Across Nations,* Thousand Oaks: Sage.

HOFSTEDE, G. 2011. *The 5D Model of professor Geert Hofstede* [Online Image]. Available: http://www.geert-hofstede.com/hofstede_dimensions.php?culture1=34&culture2=94#compare [Accessed 19 August 2011].

HUANG, C.-Y., SHEN, Y.-Z., LIN, H.-X. & CHANG, S.-S. 2007. Bloggers' Motivations and Behaviors: A Model. *Journal of Advertising Research,* 47(4), pp. 472-484.

JACKSON, N. 2006. Dipping their big toe into the blogosphere: The use of weblogs by the political parties in the 2005 general election. *Aslib Proceedings,* 58(4), pp. 292-303.

KADEN, B., KINDLING, M. & SCHULZ, M. 2007. Biblioblogsphärenklänge. Ergebnisse einer Kurzumfrage. *LIBREAS : Library Ideas,* 1+2/2007

KELLEHER, T. & MILLER, B. M. 2006. Organizational Blogs and the Human Voice: Relational Strategies and Relational Outcomes. *Journal of Computer-Mediated Communication,* 11(2), Article 1.

KLOPPE, K. 2010. State of the German Blogosphere 2010. *In:* DALE, I. (ed.) *Guide to Political Blogging in the UK.* London: Biteback.

KO, H.-C., YIN, C.-P. & KUO, F.-Y. 2008. Exploring individual communication power in the blogosphere. *Internet Research,* 18(5), pp. 541-561.

KRISHNAMURTHY, S. 2002. The multidimensionality of blog conversations: The virtual enactment of September 11. *In:* Proceedings of Internet Research 3.0, 2002 Maastricht.

LEE, C. M. & BATES, J. A. 2007. Mapping the Irish biblioblogsphere. *The Electronic Library,* 25(6), pp. 648-663.

LOMBARD, M., SNYDER-DUCH, J. & BRACKEN, C. C. 2002. Content Analysis in Mass Communication - Assessment and Reporting of Intercoder Reliability. *Human Communication Research,* 28(4), pp. 587-604.

MARANGUDAKIS, M. 2001. Rationalism and Irrationalism in the Environmental Movement—the Case of Earth First! *Democracy & Nature: The International Journal of Inclusive Democracy,* 7(3), pp. 457-467.

MISHNE, G. & GLANCE, N. 2006. Leave a Reply: An Analysis of Weblog Comments. *In:* Proceedings of the WWW2006 blog workshop, 2006 Edinburgh.

NARDI, B. A., SCHIANO, D. J., GUMBRECHT, M. & SCHWARTZ, L. 2004. Why we blog. *Communications of the ACM,* 47(12), pp. 41-46.

NEUENDORF, K. A. 2002. *The Content Analysis Guidebook,* Thousand Oaks: Sage.

OECD 2001. Environmental Country Reviews. *In:* OECD (ed.) *Environmental Performance Reviews: Germany (2001).* OECD.

OLIVER, P. 2010. *Understanding the Research Process,* London: Sage.

OTT, R. 2006. Weblogs als Medium politischer Kommunikation im Bundestagswahlkampf 2005. *In:* HOLTZ-BACHA, C. (ed.) *Die Massenmedien im Wahlkampf.* Wiesbaden: VS Verlag für Sozialwissenschaften.

PAPACHARISSI, Z. 2007. Audiences and Media Producers: Content Analysis of 260 Blogs. *In:* TREMAYNE, M. (ed.) *Blogging, Citizenship, and the Future of Media.* New York: Routledge.

PEDERSEN, S. & MACAFEE, C. 2007a. A comparison of the blogging practices of UK and US bloggers. *In:* Proceedings of ELPUB Conference on Electronic Publishing, 2007 Vienna.

PEDERSEN, S. & MACAFEE, C. 2007b. Gender Differences in British Blogging. *Journal of Computer-Mediated Communication,* 12(4), pp. 1472-1492.

PREUß, O. 2011. Die Chance der Energiewende. *Hamburger Abendblatt* [Online]. Available: http://www.abendblatt.de/wirtschaft/article1990119/Die-Chance-der-Energiewende.html [Accessed 13 August 2011].

QUICK, W. 2002. I propose a name for. *Daily Pundit* [Online]. Available from: http://dailypundit.com/?p=10823 [Accessed 08 April 2011].

RETTBERG, J. W. 2008. *Blogging,* Cambridge: Polity Press.

RIFFE, D., LACY, S. & FICO, F. 1998. *Analyzing Media Messages : Using Quantitative Content Analysis in Research* [Online]. Lawrence Erlbaum Associates, Inc. Available: http://search.ebscohost.com/login.aspx?direct=true&db=nlebk&AN=19411&site=ehost-live&scope=site [Accessed 03 August 2011].

SCHALL, H. & MÜLLER, C. 2011. Blogger – die neuen Influencer. *In:* LEINEMANN, R. (ed.) *IT-Berater und soziale Medien.* Berlin: Springer Berlin Heidelberg.

SCHÖNBERGER, K. (ed.) 2008. *Doing Gender, kulturelles Kapital und Praktiken des Bloggens,* Berlin: Hengartner.

SMITH, B. G. 2010. The evolution of the blogger: Blogger considerations of public relations-sponsored content in the blogosphere. *Public Relations Review,* 36(2), pp. 175-177.

SOBEL, J. 2010. *State of the Blogosphere 2010 Introduction* [Online]. Available: http://technorati.com/blogging/article/state-of-the-blogosphere-2010-introduction/ [Accessed 08 April 2011].

STAKE, R. 1995. *The Art of Case Study Research,* Thousand Oaks: Sage.

STERN, P. C., DIETZ, T., TROY, A., GUAGNANO, G. A. & KALOF, L. 1999. A Value-Belief-Norm Theory of Support for Social Movements: The Case of Environmentalism. *Human Ecology Review,* 6(2), pp. 81-97.

SUNDAR, S. S., EDWARDS, H. H., HU, Y. & STAVROSITU, C. 2007. Blogging for Better Health: Putting the "Public" Back in Public Health. *In:* TREMAYNE, M. (ed.) *Blogging, Citizenship, and the Future of Media.* New York: Routledge.

TGI EUROPA. 2011. TGI-Studie: Wie umweltbewusst sind europäische Verbraucher wirklich? [Online] Available: http://kantarmedia-tgide.com/2011/07/14/tgi-studie-wie-umweltbewusst-sind-europaische-verbraucher-wirklich/ [Accessed 22 August 2011].

THELWALL, M. 2006. Bloggers during the London attacks: Top information sources and topics. *In:* Proceedings of *WWW2006 blog workshop.* 2006 Edinburgh.

TORRES-ZÚÑIGA, V. 2009. Blogs as an effective tool to teach and popularize physics: a case study. *Latin American Journal of Physical Education,* 3(2), pp. 214-220.

TRAMMELL, K. D., TARKOWSKI, A., HOFMOKL, J. & SAPP, A. M. 2006. Rzeczpospolita blogów [Republic of Blog]: Examining Polish bloggers through content analysis. *Journal of Computer-Mediated Communication,* 11(3), Article 2.

TREMAYNE, M. 2007. Introduction: Examining the Blog-Media Relationship. *In:* TREMAYNE, M. (ed.) *Blogging, Citizenship, and the Future of Media.* New York: Routledge.

WEBER, L. 2009. *Marketing to the Social Web: How Digital Customer Communities Build Your Business,* Hoboken: Wiley

WINER, D. & NISENHOLTZ, M. 2002. Long Bets.[Online] Available: http://longbets.org/2/ [Accessed 07 April 2011].

WOLCOTT, H. F. 1994. *Transforming Qualitative Data: Description, Analysis, and Interpretation,* Thousand Oaks: Sage.

ZHOU, X. 2009. The political blogosphere in China: A content analysis of the blogs regarding the dismissal of Shanghai leader Chen Yiangyu. *New Media & Society,* 11(6), pp. 1003-1022.

Appendix II: Research Journal

This research journal serves as a supplement to chapter 3 about research methodology. It documents the research process in order to ensure transparency and replicability of the study. First, the chronological sequence of the research process will be briefly explained, followed by instructions for coding, which can be followed by coders during future blog research projects. Additionally, the journal explains how the blog categories were established using an adapted version of grounded theory.

i. **Chronological Research Process**

The research project started off with the choice of the topic. It was clear very early that it would deal with blogs, but the topic area had to be further narrowed down in order to balance workload and available time for the research process.

At the same time, the initial search for literature began and the author started to inform herself about previous research on blogs and identified key researchers in the field as well as relevant academic journals that would provide previous academic findings about blogs.

The topic was narrowed down to research about the environmental blogosphere in Germany and was later changed to a comparative study about the German and UK environmental blogosphere after consultation with the dissertation supervisor. The literature search was expanded to environmental movements as well and to blog research on the two countries. Eventually, the research objectives and aim evolved.

Also, the approaches of previous blog studies were looked at in order to develop a suitable research methodology. It was clear at an early stage that content analysis would be used, because it had proven of value in many previous studies and was an objective way of research.

The next issue that needed to be tackled was drawing a sample of German and UK environmental blog entries. The environmental blogosphere turned out to be rather small despite of the growing importance of environmental issues in public debates, so it was decided to arrive at a statistically valid quantity of blog entries by using multiple blog entries per blog from the top-ranked environmental blogs, since these were regularly updated and readers were engaging with them.

ii.   **Coding of Blog Entries**

Once it was clear that content analysis was the method of choice and that the sample would be drawn from the top-ranked blogs, a pilot coding scheme was developed and tested on a few blog entries. It was tested whether the coding variables delivered useful data and next to that it was recorded how much time was needed on average to code one entry. That way, a suitable amount of blog entries to code could be determined.

Some variables were changed until the last pilot study delivered acceptable results and so the coding of the whole sample, which consisted of the latest 20 blog entries of the 20 top-ranked UK and German environmental blogs, was performed. At the end, there were thus 800 coded blog entries awaiting analysis (see following section for coding instructions). The coding variables were:

- Length of blog entry
- Number of reader comments per entry
- Number of links
- Blog authors (one or multiple)
- Purpose of the blog (private or non-personal)
- Number of "I" per 1,000 words

With the results, calculations were made so that the figures and percentages could be compared between the two countries. In order to be able to have meaningful figures to compare, some variables, such as the average number of links, were calculated per 1,000 words of text instead of per blog entry.

While reading through the blog entries prior to coding, the author realised that although the broad topic of the sampled blogs was environmentalism, there seemed to be different sub-categories which were considered worthwhile researching. In order to come up with blog categories in an academically sound way, a grounded-theory approach was used.

iii. Instructions for Coding

Variable	How to Measure	Unit
Length of blog entry	Computer-automated word count, e.g. using Microsoft Word or other text-processing software. Exclude title and comments.	Words
Number of reader comments	Mostly automatically stated on the blog, if not provided count manually, including sub-comments ("comments on comments")	Comment
Number of links	Links are usually highlighted in the text or can be recognised when moving the mouse cursor over them. Exclude pictures. Only links within the text are counted.	Link (can consist of one or more words/numbers)
Blog authors	Entries usually state at the beginning who posted them. Scroll through a couple of entries to determine whether there is more than one author. If there is nothing revealed in the entries, look for an "about" page on the blog.	Number of Authors (1 or multiple)
Purpose of blog	Is there evidence for a commercial or otherwise non-personal purpose of blog? Is the author a company or a politician? Sometimes this is hidden, if necessary look at the "about" page of the blog.	Private/Non-personal
Number of "I" per 1,000 words	Merge all sampled blog entries into one document, excluding comments. Computer-automated word count of "I". Calculate: (number of "I" x 1,000)/total number of words in sample	Words

iv.   **Grounded Theory for Blog Categorisation**

The procedure of using grounded theory for generating blog categories has been described in detail in chapter 3.1.4. and will only be repeated briefly here. As required by the theory, the first step was to note down keywords for each blog entry which described its content. Afterwards, all keywords belonging to one blog were summarised into one main theme per blog before finally being grouped with similar themes from other blogs into the categories. Actually, grounded theory would consequently generate a theory from the emerged categories, but this step was omitted, because the categories were the desired result.

v.   **Drawing Conclusions**

Next to establishing categories for the environmental blogs, it was also looked at the Wikio general top20 ranking in order to find out which categories were dominant in the two countries. With that information it was possible to draw conclusions about the relative importance of the environmental blogosphere within the whole country's blogosphere. The two Wikio general rankings can be found in Appendix IV.

Finally, all data was collected and analysed statistically where possible. The next step was thus to draw conclusions from those results. The results were critically compared to what had been found out in the literature review and for those results that were different from what the literature review suggested and those that did not appear in the literature review, explanations were looked for. Some issues, such as the reasons for the higher usage of the personal pronoun "I" needed to be investigated within other academic disciplines, in this case cultural studies and linguistics.

Some of the results however, would require in-depth research and they could therefore not been looked into beyond speculations. These were noted down in chapter 6.2. about recommendations for further research.

A good piece of research also needs to acknowledge its limitations so they were included at the end of the research process, along with a reflection on the research project. These depict the last two sections of the main part of this paper.

Appendix III: Raw Data from Primary Research (per blog)

Blog #	Avg. use of "I" per 1,000 words	Avg. Length of posts	Number of comments	How many posts have comments at all?	% of non-personal blogs	% of multi author blogs	Avg. Number of links per post	% of posts without comments	Avg. Number of links per 1,000 words
1		612.55	2.90	13.00			4.05	35.00	6.61
2		507.10	14.45	13.00			4.25	35.00	8.38
3		145.45	2.35	10.00			2.95	50.00	20.28
4		109.15	1.15	9.00			3.70	55.00	33.90
5		515.45	12.15	19.00			0.70	5.00	1.36
6		468.50	3.85	17.00			7.85	15.00	16.76
7		257.05	4.70	11.00			2.00	45.00	7.78
8		280.15	2.15	5.00			11.55	75.00	41.23
9		306.95	0.85	3.00			3.45	85.00	11.24
10		493.60	0.00	0.00			7.40	100.00	14.99
11		201.70	0.30	5.00			2.00	75.00	9.92
12		422.80	1.10	11.00			8.60	45.00	20.34
13		411.15	0.00	0.00			1.55	100.00	3.77
14		437.85	0.10	2.00			3.10	90.00	7.08
15		590.90	0.60	6.00			9.70	70.00	16.42
16		326.80	0.05	1.00			1.55	95.00	4.74
17		297.20	0.60	4.00			3.85	80.00	12.95
18		256.15	1.30	10.00			1.40	50.00	5.47
19		359.15	1.50	11.00			6.45	45.00	17.96
20		425.70	0.45	7.00			4.95	65.00	11.63
Germany	5.80	371.27	2.53	7.85	40%	40%	4.55	60.75	13.64

Blog #	Avg. use of "I" per 1,000 words	Avg. Length of posts	Number of comments	How many posts have comments at all?	% of non-personal blogs	% of multi author blogs	Avg. Number of links per post	% of posts without comments	Avg. Number of links per 1,000 words
21		647.10	1.60	8.00			3.60	60.00	5.56
22		736.00	37.30	20.00			3.35	0.00	4.55
23		405.20	5.15	13.00			9.70	35.00	23.94
24		271.80	0.30	4.00			6.45	80.00	23.73
25		820.00	7.95	20.00			0.55	0.00	0.67
26		650.40	2.70	15.00			5.25	25.00	8.07
27		348.65	0.45	4.00			6.25	80.00	17.93
28		166.65	0.45	5.00			2.35	75.00	14.10
29		156.75	0.65	5.00			1.75	75.00	11.16
30		269.65	0.30	2.00			3.00	90.00	11.13
31		507.70	7.70	14.00			2.45	30.00	4.83
32		563.80	1.75	10.00			3.35	50.00	5.94
33		282.90	4.65	17.00			1.90	15.00	6.72
34		454.80	0.35	5.00			2.25	75.00	4.95
35		312.75	5.75	17.00			4.60	15.00	14.71
36		210.50	0.65	7.00			1.20	65.00	5.70
37		382.50	0.55	5.00			4.20	75.00	10.98
38		823.05	0.95	7.00			5.05	65.00	6.14
39		767.75	5.35	19.00			6.85	5.00	8.92
40		185.85	0.15	3.00			2.25	85.00	12.11
UK	9.03	448.19	4.24	10.00	60%	40%	3.82	50.00	10.09